THE CONSULTING PROCESS
AS DRAMA

THE CONSULTING PROCESS AS DRAMA

AS DRAMA

LEARNING FROM *KING LEAR*

Erik de Haan

KARNAC

LONDON   NEW YORK

English edition published in 2004 by
H. Karnac (Books) Ltd.
6 Pembroke Buildings, London NW10 6RE

First published in Dutch, *King Lear* voor adviseurs en managers:
Het adviesproces als drama, published by Scriptum Management in 1997

English translation by Corry Donner and Nico Swaan, 2004

British Library Cataloguing in Publication Data

A C.I.P. for this book is available from the British Library

ISBN 1 85575 986 1

Edited, designed, and produced by The Studio Publishing Services Ltd,
Exeter EX4 8JN

Printed in Great Britain

10 9 8 7 6 5 4 3 2 1

www.karnacbooks.com

What, in ill thoughts again? Men must endure
Their going hence even as their coming hither.
Ripeness is all. Come on.

Edgar, in: *King Lear*, V.2.9

CONTENTS

FOREWORDS   ix

PROLOGUE   xvii

Introduction   1
    a.   Key issues in consulting
    b.   Introduction to *King Lear*
    c.   The rebirth of tragedy
    d.   Who's got the monkey?

CHAPTER ONE
Exposition   7
    a.   Consulting: key issues in making an entry
    b.   *King Lear* (I.1–I.2)
    c.   Confrontation with the irresponsible
    d.   The contacting and contracting phase

CHAPTER TWO
Development   15
    a.   Consulting: key issues in stating the problem
    b.   *King Lear* (I.3–II.4)
    c.   The inescapable consequences
    d.   The diagnosis phase

CHAPTER THREE
Crisis and peripeteia   23
    a. Consulting: key issues in making a difference
    b. *King Lear* (III.1–III.7)
    c. The session on the heath
    d. The implementation phase

CHAPTER FOUR
Denouement   33
    a. Consulting: key issues in making it last
    b. *King Lear* (IV.1–IV.7)
    c. Catharsis
    d. The consolidation phase

CHAPTER FIVE
Catastrophe and exodus   41
    a. Consulting: key issues in letting go
    b. *King Lear* (V.1–V.3)
    c. Saevis tranquillus in undis
    d. The evaluation phase

Conclusion   49

EPILOGUE   55

REFERENCES   63

INDEX   65

FOREWORDS

David Armstrong

In this highly original and evocative book Erik de Haan offers a series of parallel meditations on the practice of consultancy and the tragic drama of Shakespeare's masterpiece, *King Lear*. His central theme weaves around the issue of responsibility: lost and found, denied, projected, accepted and owned. Although at times De Haan approaches the play as exemplifying the drama of consultancy, the experience of reading it is rather to set in train a dialogue between the play and the practice in which each illuminates the other. In this regard De Haan's text intriguingly mirrors the "consulting state of mind" he both seeks to address and convey. Perhaps a true measure of his success is, paradoxically, the restlessness of mind one experiences at the end of the journey—not passion spent but passion earned.

David Armstrong
Principal Consultant,
The Tavistock Consultancy Service

Bill Critchley

Erik de Haan's writing is simultaneously erudite and accessible. This is, of course, a translation, but the translators have clearly done a good job, because one has a sense of De Haan's own voice which is at once conversational and thoughtful, practical and theoretical.

King Lear is as famous as *Macbeth* or *Midsummer Night's Dream*, but probably less read and less frequently staged, so it is possible, gentle reader, that you, like me, have only a superficial acquaintance with the plot. You have no need to worry. De Haan clearly loves and knows the play well, and he unfolds the plot lucidly and simply. He also provides his own interpretations with subtlety and insight.

What I suspect is unique in his interpretation of the play, is his construction of three characters, namely the Fool, Edgar and Kent as "consultants" to Lear. Each represents a different type of relationship between client and consultant in which consultants may or may not have some transformational effect. This double parallel, one with the play, and the other with Eric Berne's "Transactional Analysis" model yielded some fruitful insights.

He also refers to Gregory Bateson's concept of complementary and symmetrical relationships, although as he does not reference

Bateson it is possible that he was, consciously at least, unaware of it. His writing is rich in the sense that there are a number of parallels and analogies working at the same time, but they are treated lightly and skilfully, so one does not experience the struggle of reading an academic treatise, while one is aware of a subtle intelligence at work.

He could have written this as a straightforward guide to consulting without the reference to Lear, which is both a strength and a weakness. The strength is that his elaboration of the nature of consulting, when he talks about consulting as "speaking one's mind", as exploration, of being with and facilitating change, is extremely useful, as is his differentiation of the different consulting roles. So any consultant coming to this text will find much insight and food for thought, whether or not he finds Lear useful as an analogy.

His linking together of the phases of the consulting process with the phases of a classical tragedy seems, however, less convincing. As he points out, plays start and finish, curtains come down between acts, and the audience finally goes home. We all know this when we arrive in the theatre. However a consulting assignment has much less sense of a "progress", and it may be unhelpful to come to an assignment with such a linear sense of phased movement. Organisational life is messily non-linear and unpredictable, and consultants who come with an over-developed sense of order may find it hard to respond to the dynamic and emergent nature of events.

Undoubtedly his weaving together of the play with consulting makes the narrative much more interesting and the play provides a rich source of insight. Whether or not you think that consulting really has the phases, the drama and intensity of a tragedy, you will of course decide for yourself.

Bill Critchley
Business Director of Ashridge Consulting

Laurence J. Gould

Whatever one may think of Erik de Haan's views and conceptual orientation, this volume is a delightful read, and quite useful in a number of ways. First, it provides an extremely valuable overview of many of the major issues in the praxis of organizational consultation. Each of the five chapters, for example, begins with a section titled "Consulting: key issues in ..." such as "making an entry"; "stating the problem", and so forth. As such, in both spirit and substance—and I do not mean this as a negative, quite the contrary—it is a serious example of the popular "everything you wanted to know genre," with the "everything" in this case, framed by the engaging, dramatic metaphor of King Lear and his "consultants" (the Fool, Edgar and Kent). This leads directly to what I think is its most useful contribution. It provokes and "irritates" in the best sense of these terms, so whether one agrees or disagrees with the views he espouses regarding any particular consultation issue, the book is a pedagogical gem, in that it cannot help but stimulate a lively debate, whether internally, with a group of colleagues, or teaching students.

Laurence J. Gould
Ph.D. Institute for Psychoanalytic Training and Research, New York

Roger Harrison

I really liked this book. Ashridge Consulting's Erik de Haan has captured the essence of the consultant–client relationship by means of a gracefully choreographed dance between deep reflections on his own experience, and Shakespeare's play, *King Lear*. I have never read such an elegantly literate exposition of the nuances of the consulting process. Dr De Haan presents a robust model of the issues and choices that arise for the consultant, and brilliantly interweaves well-chosen passages from *King Lear* to exemplify the model. Not only is this a book to delight the philosophically inclined among us, but it beautifully illustrates De Haan's down to earth approach to consulting. After forty years of consulting practice, I found insights into consultant–client relationships that had previously escaped me. De Haan's approach is highly practical; if we were to follow it more closely, we and our clients would both profit thereby.

Not least, this is a short and succinct book, and De Haan's message is conveyed without over-elaboration and with real artistry. Moreover, the translation from the Dutch by Corry Donner and Nico Swaan is excellent.

Roger Harrison
Organization Development Consultant and Writer

Dr Peter Hawkins

There is a plethora of books on Management, Leadership and Consultancy adding to the mountain of knowledge about these subjects. Hakim Sanni, the great Sufi poet wrote, "Knowledge without Wisdom is like an unlit candle." What is needed and what is in short supply is not repetitive knowledge, but real wisdom about the consulting process. Where better to search for wisdom than in the great treasure chest of Shakespeare's plays and it is to one of the most wise of Shakespeare's plays that Erik de Haan takes us. *King Lear*, the play in which the old King is struggling to move from leader to elder, from control to enabling others. But Lear mistakes eldership for abdication, and he manages his succession as a reward to those who voice love for him

Erik de Haan uses Lear's journey to illustrate the many stages of the consulting process: entry, stating the problem, making a difference, making the change sustainable and managing exit. Throughout the book and again in his epilogue he shows how a central theme runs throughout these stages and the course of the play. This is the theme of taking the appropriate responsibility and having the appropriate mandate, so that responsibility and mandate are commensurate.

He also shows up a deeper theme about the process that Lear has to endure: a process of unlearning and being reduced to nothing, so that he can learn that you can truly make use of nothing. By losing all that he holds most dear and being driven to the edge of sanity he develops some "negative capabilities", necessary for both true eldership and effective consulting. For as consultants we must be responsible not only for what we do, but also for choosing when not to act, not to speak and when not to take responsibility.

The great twentieth century polymath, Gregory Bateson, wrote:

Rigour alone is paralytic death, but imagination alone is insanity. (*Mind and Nature*, p. 233)

De Haan has given us a book that weaves rigour and imagination to illuminate the consultant's journey, which may not be as dramatic as Lear's but has as many challenges.

Dr Peter Hawkins
Chairman of Bath Consultancy Group

PROLOGUE

This book gives a summary of key issues in management consulting, in a step by step, chronological way. However, it is directed mainly at those consultants who know from experience that consulting does not work as smoothly as the manuals suggest, and who have learned through trials and tribulations to take a tragic outlook on the art of consulting.

In a consulting situation, the client shares a story with the consultant. If this story deals with important themes and if there are problems as well, it quickly embodies the elements of a dramatic situation and may even assume the proportions of a drama. Having an eye for the dramatic in a client's situation can be advantageous for a consultant. In this book I will try to shed light upon these issues with the help of a drama that is highly relevant to gaining an understanding of consulting, leadership, and management: Shakespeare's *King Lear*. The central theme of *King Lear*, I will argue, is responsibility.

Responsibility is also one of the cornerstones of a successful consulting process, together with empathy and trust (Block, 1981). Responsibility differentiates itself from the other two cornerstones in that "more" is not always "better". The assumption of too much responsibility by the consultant may, for instance, lead to a loss of autonomy on the part of the client. The objective is to achieve a delicate balance of shared responsibility.

The consulting process is frequently divided into five phases (Bell & Nadler, 1979; Block, 1981). These bear a striking resemblance to the five phases of a classical tragedy. In the consulting process the phases are:

1. Contacting and contracting.
2. Diagnosis.
3. Implementation.
4. Consolidation.
5. Evaluation.

The five phases of a classical tragedy are usually described as (Bradley, 1904):

1. Exposition.
2. Development.
3. Crisis and peripeteia.
4. Denouement.
5. Catastrophe and exodus.

These five phases are not always rigidly adhered to either in management consulting or in drama. However, there is already something tragic in the unavoidability of these most basic phases, as every process has a definite beginning, middle, and end. Although many modern dramatists, beginning with Beckett, have tried to break free from classical phasing, they still find themselves with a beginning, some sort of development, and an end, if only for the fact that the public will want to know when to arrive at the theatre, and that the programme will end before the onset of night. The same applies to management consulting: in spite of heroic attempts to put the end at the beginning or to conceive of a circular process by means of approaches such as simulations and action research cycles, a consulting intervention remains a time-bounded collaborative relationship with a beginning, middle, and end.

I will discuss beginning, middle, and end in terms of the five classical phases summarized above, with reference to:

(a) key issues in the art of consulting;
(b) the tragedy *King Lear* as a case study;

(c) Lear, his advisers and the theme of responsibility;

(d) a tragic, or at least dramatic, perspective on consulting.

Each chapter of the book is composed in this way, such that it reads as a general introduction to some key issues in consulting, followed by a dramatic intermezzo in the reading of *King Lear*, and finally a deepening into the more dramatic aspects of the art of consulting. The four essays that result from this division may also be read independently of each other. An introduction precedes each of the four.

What may the reader expect to find in the following pages? At the very least, a great deal of drama and tension, on the one hand in a tragedy in which eight of the twelve main characters die of unnatural causes, and, on the other hand, in a sound and well-structured consulting process. It will become clear that, perhaps surprisingly, there are many positive lessons to be learned from the tragedy of *King Lear*, for both the manager and the management consultant. However tragically the play ends, *King Lear* can be viewed as a very successful consulting intervention: the king undergoes a profound change that enables him to better understand his own situation, to accept it and to improve upon it.

Introduction

a. Key issues in consulting

I define the art of management consulting as "a temporary collaborative relationship between a client or organization and a consultant, the objective of which is an improvement in the client's fortunes". This definition gives the art of consulting a time boundary and therefore a beginning, middle, and end—even some kind of directionality. In short it turns consulting into a *process* which can, and in this book will be, divided up into phases. However, as much as this "process approach" may clarify the art of consulting, it may also obscure the essence of it. It is with this process as with time itself according to St Augustine (398): "I know well enough what it is, provided that nobody asks me; but if I am asked what it is and try to explain, I am baffled". And when St Augustine concludes a little later, "neither the past nor the future exists; they exist in the mind at present, but nowhere else that I can see", the same could be said for the consulting process.

Consulting is much more like a state of mind in the present than it is like a process. This state of mind has a number of aspects that will serve as key perspectives on consulting in each of the chapters that follow. In these chapters the aspects will seem to fit quite well with the particular phase of the process, but in truth they are very much part of the single, multi-faceted stone that consulting is. This means that everything mentioned below as being a "key issue" for that particular phase can also be viewed as a key issue for consulting, regardless of the particular phase of the consulting relationship.

The different aspects that will be stressed in the following chapters are:

1. Consulting is "speaking one's mind" openly and truly—without fear of the consequences.
2. Consulting is exploration—listening to and interpreting whatever the client brings.
3. Consulting is self-monitoring and self-directing—the ability to view one's actions while one performs these same actions from a different, more objective perspective.
4. Consulting is being with and facilitating change—respecting the autonomous and independent nature of that change.
5. Consulting is letting go of the client and the client's fortunes—practising detachment *vis-à-vis* the change that, as a consultant, one has personally become involved in.

It has perhaps crossed some readers' minds that "giving advice" is not part of these five key aspects of consulting. This is deliberate: I do not think that giving advice should belong to the five, or, indeed, any number of key aspects of consulting.

There is a natural flow in these five definitions, where each seems to follow from the previous and each seems to be best fitted to the advance that has been made in the consulting relationship. Having said that, it is my conviction that every one of these aspects of consulting is present if one is in the "consulting state of mind".

So how does one enter this state of mind that is consulting? My answer is, by noting what takes place at every single moment in the relationship with the client. If one can be fully aware of what is going on here and now and note it, one is, whether one realizes it or not, practising the art of consulting.

b. *Introduction to* King Lear

King Lear, which was written *c.* 1605 in Shakespeare's mature period, is one of his best-known tragedies and one of his most popular plays with both performers and audiences. As in Shakespeare's other great tragedies, *Macbeth, Othello*, and *Hamlet*, *King Lear* relates the story of the downfall of a king: an event so disastrous that most main characters are dragged down with him.

The story of *King Lear* appears erratic; it is full of unexpected and unanticipated turns of events. In spite of this unusual structure, in the theatre the play manifests an overwhelming unity in which all events seem both necessary and inevitable. This effect is achieved by the fact that most of the main characters struggle with similar issues, which they discuss with each other constantly. To put it in musical terms, in *King Lear* it is not the *melody*—the narrative structure—which stands out, but rather the *harmony*: the simultaneous voices of related themes. Even in its monolithic unity, the tragedy of *King Lear* presents itself as a gem with countless facets. It contains an abundance of recurring metaphors regarding nature versus civilization and autonomy versus predestination, expressed in terms of nothing versus numbers; eyes and perception; breath and speech; dressing/undressing/changing, etc.

In the following sections I will try to uncover the underlying unity in the harmonious structure of *King Lear*. The reader should take note, however, that such an interpretation can never do full justice to the play's wealth of images and symbols. For, as Verhagen (1928) says:

> this is truly the most complexly construed drama in world literature, a masterwork of composition in which two complete tragedies are intertwined, and in which almost every character, in whatever relationship he stands to the main action, achieves dramatic independence. Each meets his own fate as a direct consequence of his actions and thus becomes, at some point, a protagonist in his own right. It is like a complete polyphonic orchestral performance of a major double fugue.

Important themes in *King Lear* that receive minimal attention in the following text are the (un)conditional nature of love and forgiveness, and the recovery of the soul through the loss of the world.

c. The rebirth of tragedy

In the cradle of our Western civilization lies the birth of tragedy. The Greek tragedies of the great poets Aeschylus, Sophocles, and Euripides originated in the annual festivals in honour of the god Dionysus, in a period (550–400 BC) in which Athenian civilization flourished in an unprecedented manner. During that period the Greeks, with their tremendous faith in the human mind (*logos*), developed and organized their society in an as yet unequalled way. The tragedies may be seen as an outcome of the dramatic insights which this development stimulated. In the tragedies, the dangers of having an overly high opinion of one's own abilities were pointed out to the cultured Athenian audience. The central theme of Attic tragedy is *hybris* or "pride", meaning: claiming to be greater than what one's own limitations permit. The consequences of *hybris* are terrible: Greek gods punish without mercy those who are unaware of their own shortcomings.

Not before the sixteenth century do the tragedies of Christopher Marlowe and—more notably—William Shakespeare equal the standards set by the ancient Greeks. The great sense of confidence in the human mind (*ratio*), which characterizes the Renaissance, lies once again at the foundation of an unparalleled blossoming of society and culture. And once again, in the tragedies conceit—or a single fatal flaw—in otherwise very capable personalities, usually in a powerful king, leads to general destruction.

Shakespeare is the epitome of the Renaissance man who professes the ideal of "civilization" in all his works. Shakespeare's civilized man knows how to temper his passions and is able to understand and accept his place in the social order. In other words, Shakespeare continually advocates good husbandry: the ability to accept the responsibilities that attach to a given (social) role.

King Lear approaches the classical theme of pride in an original way: from the beginning of the play, King Lear wants nothing but an unburdened crawl toward death (I.1.41) and he maintains this trait of renunciation, this longing to be left in peace, until the end. From the opening scene of the play, it is clear that Lear, in abdicating his responsibilities as the King of England, suffers from "lack of pride", which, like *hybris*, constitutes a serious offence against one's own fate.

d. Who's got the monkey?

Contemporary society is rapidly becoming extremely complex. In every social arena, there are complicated systems of rules and procedures, for which very specialized knowledge is needed. Management is assuming an ever more central role, and the knowledge-intensive services (legal, accounting, and consulting) are experiencing a golden era. It is no longer possible to lead an organization without hiring expert knowledge.

Of the professions that render knowledge-intensive services, that of the management consultant is no doubt the most controversial, because the management consultant deals with what is the very essence of the job of his client: managing the organization. (For the sake of convenience, I shall use only the male form for consultants and their clients in all generic statements.) Perhaps the spectacular growth of the management consultancy sector is in part due to a flight, on the part of senior management in many organizations, from their own responsibilities. If this is so then it is clearly essential that the responsibilities of both the client and the consultant within the consulting process be clearly defined. Especially in the case of "dramatic" situations, marked by dilemmas or conflicts that have a profound impact on the functioning of all concerned, the client may attempt to shift his own responsibilities on to the consultant's shoulders. In such cases, it is as well to have learned from *King Lear* about the serious consequences that may arise from the abdication of responsibilities.

The phenomenon of passing responsibility on to others is well known in management literature. Oncken and Wass (1974) coined the analogy of "the leap of the monkey", with the monkey being the problem which an employee attempts to pass on to his manager. But beware: as soon as the monkey is on the manager's back, the employee no longer has a problem, and hence the manager can no longer advise him! The same fate can befall the unwary consultant.

That Shakespeare's *King Lear*, more so than *Hamlet*, *Othello*, or *Macbeth*, deals with issues found in management and consulting is reflected in the language used in the play: words such as *manage*, *lead*, *advise*, *counsel*, and *comfort* appear in *King Lear* much more frequently than in the other tragedies.

Much has been written about the consulting process, and I do not intend to revisit all that material here. My emphasis is on the division of responsibilities between consultant and client. In particular, attention will be focused on situations and circumstances in which the consultant is truly tested. However, it is not my intention to suggest that a consulting process always follows a dramatic or tragic course: in my experience most assignments run their course smoothly and in mutual agreement.

CHAPTER ONE

Exposition

a. Consulting: key issues in making an entry

I n the first phase of consulting, which mainly deals with
contacting and contracting, the establishment of a consulting
relationship can be viewed as an underlying aim. The question
is whether it is at all possible to reach the kind of collaborative
relationship that is needed for consulting to begin.

Experience shows that usually the entry "starts before it starts":
both the client and the consultant have images and expectations of
the other, even before they meet. Both the client's organization and
the consultant's profession usually bring with them strong
preconceptions and associations. There is no such thing as a
"neutral beginning". Let us think of the example of going to the
theatre to watch a play. We have usually heard about the play
beforehand, perhaps discussed it with people who have been before
us, or read a review. When the actual first contact takes place, first
impressions prove to be quite strong and persistent. For the
consultant, the business of finding out what belongs to the client
or to the client organization and what belongs to the consultant's
own preconceptions and biases, which is an important part of

exploration, starts from the very first contact.

In the initial contact with the client, the consultant is often struck by:

- the sudden onset of the work, with problem and problem holder presenting themselves simultaneously;
- the manifold interrelated issues, many of which are only communicated indirectly;
- the reciprocal assessment that takes place, in which the client assesses the consultant for reliability, personal power, expertise, and experience; and the consultant assesses the client for reliability and the problem situation as presented, as well as scanning for other stakeholders and problem owners;
- the difficulty in remaining "authentic" for both client and consultant, in view of the amount of "impression management" that the situation favours.

Despite all these issues, the consultant should approach the entry situation as neutrally as possible, trying to free himself from preconceptions and biases, as well as from any self-serving desire to move forward. Examples of a few questions that, asked in a neutral tone, would be useful starting points for the conversation are:

- What can I do for you?
- What brings you here?
- What shall we discuss?
- Please, feel free to commence ...

After posing one of these, the consultant will listen, summarize, and structure whatever may come up.

A successful initial contact allows the consultant to draw up a contract. The contract boils down to:

- a mutual agreement on a statement of the problem, keeping open as many options as possible;
- a psychological commitment between client and consultant;
- a list of conditions, which are meant to enable collaboration during the consulting process, in terms of mutual responsibilities and roles.

In this first phase of the process, "consulting" is established. As we will see from the examples mentioned in the following paragraphs, consulting is not a form of rhetoric, and it is not flattery. Consulting can be most closely associated with "speaking one's mind", which is the ancient concept of *parrhesia* (Foucault, 1985) and is sometimes called "being authentic" (Block, 1981). Consulting often starts with a summary of what the client brings, which can be daring enough if the client's emotions and approach towards his problem are also summarized.

The following are some aspects of consulting that will be considered in this chapter.

- The anxieties that accompany the fact that the client is seeking a consultant: he has been unable to cope with the problem on his own.
- The difficulty of disentangling the problem from the problem holder.
- The difficulty of identifying all the relevant issues pertinent to the problem, as a result of either inability or unwillingness.
- The repercussions for third parties who are not present at the contracting stage.

b. King Lear (I.1–I.2)

DRAMATIS PERSONÆ

LEAR, King of Britain
GONERIL, Lear's eldest daughter
Duke of ALBANY, her husband
REGAN, Lear's second daughter
Duke of CORNWALL, her husband
CORDELIA, Lear's youngest daughter
King of FRANCE suitors of Cordelia
Duke of BURGUNDY
Earl of KENT, later disguised as Caius
Earl of GLOUCESTER

EDGAR, elder son of Gloucester,
later disguised as Tom o' Bedlam
EDMUND, bastard son of Gloucester
OLDMAN, Gloucester's tenant
CURAN, Gloucester's retainer
Lear's FOOL
OSWALD, Goneril's steward
A doctor, a herald, a captain,
gentlemen, servants, knights,
soldiers, messengers

It is clear from the very start of *King Lear* that a division of the kingdom is imminent. One wonders which of his sons-in-law will prove to be Lear's favourite, the Duke of Albany or the Duke of Cornwall? When Lear himself enters the stage, he would like to know which of his daughters loves him most: *Which of you shall we say doth love us most?* (I.1.51). The two eldest, Goneril and Regan, gladly join in the game and start flattering the King brazenly to secure their part of the kingdom. Not so Cordelia. Cordelia merely states who she is, Lear's daughter, and that she has nothing more and nothing less to offer than that which is in accordance with that bond. Her words obviously do not meet Lear's expectations and he immediately expels her, in spite of his lamentation that:

> I loved her most, and thought to set my rest
> On her kind nursery. [I.1.122]

The Earl of Kent stands up for Cordelia and presents Lear with the essential facts of the matter:

1. Power bows to flattery.
2. A decision is being taken rashly.
3. Cordelia's love for her father is being grossly underestimated.

Lear does not want to be criticized; he expels Kent from his kingdom as well. He now unceremoniously presents Cordelia to her rival suitors, the Duke of Burgundy and the King of France, yet without a dowry. Burgundy is no longer interested, but France all the more so, resulting in Cordelia's departure for the mainland. She coolly bids her sisters goodbye. Her farewell is followed by a tête-à-tête between Goneril and Regan who patronizingly declare their surprise at the infirmity of old age: Lear always loved Cordelia most and now he has cast her off ... yet: *he hath ever but slenderly known himself* (I.1.292).

Lear remains king in name only and keeps some one hundred men in his train. He intends to live with his two eldest daughters, staying a month with each, by turns.

Simultaneously, in the first two scenes, the audience is introduced to another plot that centres on the Earl of Gloucester and his two sons: Edgar and the bastard son Edmund. Throughout the play, this story functions as a mirror to Lear's story, deepening and expanding on the themes presented in the latter. Gloucester will lose his county to Edmund, whose intrigues start when he hands to his father a false and treacherous letter, allegedly written by Edgar, leading Gloucester to believe that it is Edgar who is after his inheritance. At the same time, Edmund ensures that his elder half-brother Edgar lives in fear of Gloucester's anger.

c. Confrontation with the irresponsible

In the first scene, the audience sees an old and irritable, yet impulsively decisive king appear on stage, a king who appears more interested in the love people feel for him than in governing his state. He wants to give up the latter immediately, and offers his state to the daughter who claims to love him most.

For someone with a task like Lear's—to rule the English nation and to raise three daughters—turning the state into an emotional bribe for the daughters is indeed an irresponsible action. As we shall see, the consequences prove disastrous to both the stability of the kingdom and Lear's personal life.

Lear's self-knowledge is still limited at this point. This is literally stated but also appears from a contrast effect in the exposition, apparent in the large number of people who do introduce themselves demonstratively. The king compensates for his lack of self-knowledge with a virtually insatiable need for the affirmation of those around him: people have to like him and if they don't he explodes into wild fits of rage.

Lear's highest wisdom, which he expresses twice (I.1.90 and I.4.131), is the nihilistic *Nothing can be made out of nothing*. In the course of the tragedy he will be reduced to nothing in order to learn that it is just this that enables him to gain new, essential insights. However, this is not yet the case and the King has grown old before he has grown wise. The Fool tells him so in 1.5.38:

If thou wert my Fool, nuncle, I'd have thee beaten for being old
before thy time [...]
Thou shouldst not have been old till thou hadst been wise.

Closer inspection of the introduction of Gloucester and his sons shows that Edgar makes a very bland impression in the exposition: Edgar becomes a true character only after his flight and chase in the second Act. At this point, he is still an easy prey for the intrigues of his half-brother Edmund, or put in the latter's words, he is

... a brother noble,
Whose nature is so far from doing harms
That he suspects none; on whose foolish honesty
My practices ride easy. [I.2.175]

Our acquaintance with the main characters ends in both stories with a contractual settlement:

(a) Lear will stay with Goneril and Regan, by turns, for one month at a time with his train of one hundred men, while retaining his honour and the dignity of king.
(b) Edmund settles Edgar's fate with the fake note that he holds under Gloucester's nose.

d. The contacting and contracting phase

The first moment of contact between a consultant and a potential client is an extremely important one in the consulting process: first impressions are not easily changed. In a way, too many things happen at once at that moment: the client tries to assess the consultant (reliability, personal power, expertise, experience), while the consultant assesses the client (reliability, problem situation as presented, stakeholders and problem owners). Both the client and the consultant are occupied with the impression they are making on the other person, simultaneously assessing to what extent their working together is feasible and appealing. Moreover, the consultant knows that if anything goes wrong in this phase, either he will not be given the assignment or he will regret the mistakes further down the road. The purpose of contact for both parties is to arrive at a contract, to enter into a business agreement which satisfies both parties. The contract is a "psychological contract" in which the *responsibilities* of client and consultant are sharply defined. Therefore, everything is geared to clarifying mutual expectations.

Where is the drama in this phase?

Generally speaking, people only ask for advice when they know they cannot cope on their own. That is why tension is high from the very first moment of contact. The opening of a consulting assignment shows striking similarities to the opening of a play: the client is "king", and he suddenly appears before us and acts. Often, the (formal) responsibility of the person we meet is of a high level, while his insight into the origin and development of the problem is of a lower level. We encounter not only the person asking advice, but also his problem, which, in word and action, is still undistinguishable from the person. Moreover, it is unlikely that the entire problem will be put on the table at this point: the client may have many reasons not to disclose all the relevant issues. Yet we do not have time to get better acquainted on neutral ground. On the contrary, we may want to move forward towards a contract that will enable us to get started.

The contract, as mentioned, mainly lists the responsibilities of each party. For instance, the consultant undertakes to provide a problem analysis and an improvement plan, and the client offers cooperation in terms of sharing information and committing to implement the necessary changes.

Besides this division of responsibilities, both parties are responsible for the fate of third parties: a contract may have serious consequences for others within the organization, for example a department which is performing inadequately in the eyes of the client. Both consultant and client are free to reconsider the psychological contract. However, as becomes clear in *King Lear* when Goneril immediately tries to change the contract with Lear, this may lead to strong reactions on the part of the other party. The real art is to keep options open in the contracting phase.

CHAPTER TWO

Development

a. Consulting: key issues in stating the problem

I n the second phase of the consulting assignment, the consultant has moved on from the initial contact. He has established some kind of a relationship with the main client and has ideally put a contract into place. The consultant's attention will shift slightly and his task will become more focused, as the exploration which began during the first meeting with the client will now become the exclusive aim of his efforts.

Similar to the entry phase, the exploration phase tends to "start before it starts". During the initial contact there have been first impressions and there have been first statements of the problem; now these impressions will diversify, as the consultant meets and interviews other stakeholders, and he hears other, perhaps contrary, statements of the problem. There is a gradual development from entry to exploration.

If the first phase was working towards consulting, the second phase is primarily a kind of "hovering" over consulting. There may be some pressure on the consultant to consult, but at the same time this is felt to be rather premature. One of the difficulties is how to get out of the "assessing" stance that was unavoidable when a consulting contract still had to be established. Some consultants tend to continue assessing and displaying their expert knowledge, by which they jump past this phase and run the risk of offering more straightforward consulting than tends to be helpful at this stage.

Exploration is a skill and an activity as much as a state of mind. Every consultant will have his own exploratory state of mind—and from observing different consultants we can easily distinguish different approaches. One approach is that of examination, where objectivity and predictability is high and the consultant may be seen "ticking boxes". Another is that of diagnosis, which is strongly oriented towards the problem and the difficulties at hand. A third, and somewhat contrary, approach is that of appreciative inquiry, where the consultant tries to establish what is currently working well and what can be a basis for further improvement. A fourth approach is to simply experience what is there, remaining as much as possible in the present and trying consistently to offer the client centrality, to listen and be aware of what the client is offering.

The choice of approach depends very much on the role that the consultant has contracted for (some distinct consulting roles are reviewed in the next chapter). Generally, for more difficult problems, where one wishes to remain in this phase and undertake as full an exploration as possible, it is best to opt for the fourth, most exploratory approach. The other approaches tend to have an interventional aspect, the consultant already having decided what he wants to listen to most, be it certain pre-defined categories in examination, the "bad news" in diagnosis, or the "good news" in appreciative inquiry. In practice, it turns out to be quite difficult just to simply experience together with the client. Judgements, memories, and wishes tend to pop up continuously in the consciousness of the consultant. It requires a great deal of training to be able to be fully present and explore whatever the client brings.

If one looks at the beginnings of different consulting assignments, they appear to have something in common. This commonality is an insoluble internal contradiction. In all presenting problems something undesirable, that cannot easily be undone, is the matter, or something desirable, which cannot easily be achieved, is not the matter. It may be a strategy or a habit that is adopted and cannot be stopped, or some externally enforced change, like a takeover, that has become a reality but is very difficult to work with. In the case of King Lear, this internal contradiction is of course the wish to remain king while shedding the responsibilities of being king. Matching this, the consultant will feel at this stage a similar internal contradiction, which is very difficult to disentangle, between the need to empathize with the client's misfortunes and the need to observe and analyse the client from an external perspective.

While entering into a relationship with a consultant, the client generally experiences a similar internal contradiction. He experiences himself as being in the hands of another person who supposedly knows better than himself, which puts him in an awkward position of dependency. So while on the one hand the consultant offers the promise of a way out or of a resolution, on the other hand the consulting relationship offers dependency, an undesirable nuisance to most people, even if that is not always acknowledged consciously.

The following are some aspects of consulting that will be considered in this chapter:

- the seemingly inescapable nature of the fortunes of the client;
- the contradictory nature of the presenting problem;
- the risk of getting carried away by exaggerated sympathy;
- the risk of getting carried away into assessing and judging as an outsider;
- possible reservations on the part of the client about engaging with the consultant, and pressure for results;
- the consultant feeling a kind of "tragic impotence": the client has been unable to deal with this situation, so how and why should the consultant be able to deal with it?

b. King Lear (I.3–II.4)

Goneril is the first to receive King Lear. She instantly arranges for a rude awakening as she tells her servants not to pay too much heed to the old king. Loyal Kent, who is aware of the powerless position Lear has put himself in, dons a disguise so that he can continue to serve Lear but under a different name (Caius). Lear does not see through the disguise and instructs Kent on how to interact: *Thou serv'st me, and I'll love thee* (I.4.87). The other person Lear can fall back on is his Fool, who calls a spade a spade when offering his advice to the King. Goneril comes to Lear with the arrogantly formal suggestion that he send away half his train because his men are misbehaving in her house. Lear is entirely perplexed by this admonition coming as it does from a daughter who had professed to be so loving. He swears and stamps his feet like a child, curses Goneril, and rests his hope on his second daughter Regan.

Regan is informed of the breach between Lear and his eldest daughter by letters from Goneril, through Oswald, Goneril's servant, and by letters from Lear through the Earl of Kent. She is on her way to Gloucester's castle with her husband, the Duke of Cornwall, but the two messengers arrive first. As they arrive, the sycophantic Oswald, who was rude to the old Lear earlier at Goneril's behest, is treated to an unparalleled barrage of abuse by Kent. Kent calls Oswald a vile flatterer and a *super-serviceable* lackey (II.2.18). Alarmed by the shouting, Regan, Cornwall and Gloucester come running to the scene. Kent declares:

> No contraries hold more antipathy
> Than I and such a knave [II.2.85]

Regan punishes Kent by putting him in the stocks shortly after his arrival. From this it is clear that Regan will choose her elder sister's side in the other, royal conflict. When King Lear arrives, finds his servant in the stocks, and learns that Regan and Cornwall cannot receive him because they are tired, he becomes so infuriated that his host Gloucester leaves to fetch Regan and Cornwall anyway. Regan immediately employs an imperial and patronizing tone in her words to Lear. Using *state* as a pun, she tells him:

> [...] You should be ruled and led
> By some discretion that discerns your state
> Better than yourself [II.4.145]

With a tremendous effort Lear manages to hold back his anger: he begs Regan for charity and flatters her with her *tender-hefted nature* (II.4.169). However, when Goneril arrives unexpectedly, this paper-thin trust is broken. Regan and Goneril together complete Lear's ultimate humiliation, always with cool and distant rationalizations. Lear breaks into furious yet impotent threats of revenge. The only options he feels he has are to weep or go mad. Although a violent storm erupts, Lear has his horse saddled. Cornwall, in his cruel, cynical comment that *'T is best to give him way. He leads himself* (II.4.296), emphasizes that at this point the King cannot even lead himself.

The "Gloucester plot" also runs its unstoppable course: the gullible Earl of Gloucester is easily led by Edmund to believe that Edgar wants to kill him. Edmund also makes sure that Edgar flees from the castle, so that father and son cannot speak to each other. Gloucester can do nothing but organize the pursuit of his son, and Edgar, the fugitive, who sees his position, aspirations and future at the court reduced to nothing in one single moment, decides *To take the basest and most poorest shape* (II.3.7). He tears off his clothes, smears his face with mud and turns into "Poor Tom", a miserable beggar. In this role his playful creativity will be taken to great heights, and he rightly concludes that, now that things are as they are: *That's something yet; Edgar I nothing am* (II.3.21).

c. The inescapable consequences

The drama has now developed to such an extent that we, the audience, can distinguish the main characters and can understand which of their mistakes, such as Lear's avoidance behaviour, Gloucester's gullibility, and both men's susceptibility to flattery, have led to the start of the tragedy. At the same time, the protagonists are faced with the consequences of their deeds and their fortunes are rapidly turning.

In spite of his misery, King Lear is now in the fortunate position that he has two advisers who are very different, yet who both demonstrate great integrity. The Earl of Kent and the Fool dare tell him the truth about his actions. Kent is a zealous and loyal servant to Lear, while at the same time taking the liberty of addressing Lear with the informal "thou" in the first scene of the play, thereby emphasizing his assumption of equality. Kent remains correct and businesslike under all circumstances. In his introduction in I.4.32 he defines his consulting practice as follows:

> I can keep honest counsel, ride, run, mar a curious tale in telling it,
> and deliver a plain message bluntly. That which ordinary men are
> fit for, I am qualified in; and the best of me is diligence.

This is in stark contrast, not only to Oswald, who seems in every
way to be the complete converse of a professional consultant, but
also to the Fool, who adopts humour in his treatment of the King
(Rose, 1969), speaks in riddles and shocks everyone with his
surrealistic views of events. Moreover, the Fool reflects on the issues
at a deeper level. He does not fail to notice the turnabout that Lear
causes by giving his kingdom to his flattering daughters and by
then delivering himself over to them: the tragedy begins *e'er since
thou madest thy daughters thy mothers* (I.4.168) or *when the cart draws
the horse* (I.4.221). The Fool also addresses Lear in an informal way,
even though he calls him *nuncle* (mine uncle), a word that expresses
some respect for the superior position. Lear calls the Fool *my boy*, a
complement to nuncle.

As yet, Lear does little with the major consulting talents in his
immediate environment. He does not yet understand that by
abdicating responsibility for his own destiny he also relinquishes his
honour and his prestige. He will now have to accept as his superiors
those whom he himself nurtured. The Fool puts it in rhyme:

> Fathers that wear rags
>   Do make their children blind,
> But fathers that bear bags
>   Shall see their children kind. [II.4.46]

His daughters' indifference comes as a complete surprise, and he
does not know how to react other than by throwing tantrums.

d. The diagnosis phase

The consultant starts his examination of the (client) organization.
This examination is very different from scientific research, primarily
in that objectivity is not the main goal. On the contrary, this
examination is of a purely subjective nature. The very reason the
consultant has been called in is for his personal experience and
judgement (Block, 1981). Nevertheless, just as in scientific research,

an open-minded and conscientious attitude is assumed: information is checked, interpretations are compared and evaluated, and the formulation of a position or a final opinion is delayed. Ultimately, this diagnosis is directed towards action: which will improve the fortunes of the client.

Where is the drama in this phase?

Once we have spent some time studying the problem, we will experience a certain inevitability. Before we understand exactly how the situation has come to be, we sense the inescapable patterns that lie at the root of events. We think: "With circumstances like that, this problem simply *had* to arise".

Any cynicism or pent-up anger on the part of the client that seemed surprising to us in the contacting phase, gradually becomes understandable. Now, the consultant has to refrain from empathizing too greatly with those feelings, otherwise he runs the risk of being carried away and becoming a party to vested interests himself. As a participant in the process he would become part of the system, while his expertise has been called in for the very reason that he can examine the system from the vantage point of an independent position within that system.

Pressure can come from various sides to "solve the problem". Though the consultant's examination is intended to result in an intervention in the system, he would be wise to delay action until he has obtained sufficient information.

In the meantime, as a professional he will be required to live up to the image of solidity, reliability, and expertise that he established in the contacting phase. Kent puts it succinctly in the brilliant contacting interview that he, as Caius, has with Lear (I.4.12): *I do profess to be no less than I seem.*

The responsibility of the consultant, therefore, lies in not being dragged into the tragedy, in remaining independent, and in maintaining his own professional and personal standards.

CHAPTER THREE

Crisis and peripeteia

a. Consulting: key issues in making a difference

I t is in the third phase of the consulting assignment that the consultant will become most conscious of his own contribution. The aim of consulting seems now to be to make the consultant's impact visible. One reason for this is that he will have to take a more central stance, as this is generally the phase where the consultant intervenes most. Another reason is that a lot of exploration has been undertaken; the client and the client organization will naturally turn their attention to the consultant to see what he thinks or does.

The client's expectation, or rather fantasy, is often that the consultant will now really make a difference, that the consultant will intervene and offer advice which will then solve the problem at hand. In the case of real and persisting problems, however, which have been created slowly and consistently and which have become part of the organization's structure and culture, solving the problem is not straightforward and easy. Any intervention by the consultant can easily be distorted or displaced, so that, instead of removing or alleviating the existing problems, they will exacerbate them. The consultant, who is conscious of an organization's capacity to render harmless outside interventions, will think differently about "making a difference". This consultant knows that in order to make a difference within a consulting relationship one often needs to make an unexpected move. In this relationship, making a difference changes the relationship itself. For this reason, this is generally the phase in which the client–consultant relationship is tested most, either as a result of conventional interventions that have not worked, or as a result of more daring, relationship-changing interventions that have.

The kind of difference that a consultant makes differs immensely with the kind of role he is contracted for, or chooses to take on. Usually, in the literature, some three or four roles are distinguished. Following Kolb's learning cycle (Kolb, 1984; De Haan, 2001), these are as follows:

1. The *expert*: this consultant is expected to contribute expert advice and high-level knowledge. For this reason, the expert consultant is usually largely in control of the assignment, and the level of collaboration between client and consultant is low and unidirectional (from consultant to client). To put it in somewhat stronger words, the client's contribution is only to evaluate retrospectively, while the consultant is expected to "solve" the problems. The two roles are therefore strongly complementary.

2. The *process manager*: this consultant mainly influences the relationship between the client and his problem. The consultant intervenes largely on the conditions for working through a problem. The consultant leads a project in which the client organization is going to work on its own problems. The consultant helps to bring in experts or new learning, if required, but is himself neither an expert nor a trainer. The process manager is very active and "hands on", and his relationship with the client is close and symmetrical.

3. The *trainer*: this consultant contributes to the learning of the client by offering challenging experiences, simulations, or skills training. The consultant encourages the client to approach problems differently and facilitates conditions for learning by offering a range of experiences. The consultant–client relationship is generally close and complementary, with the client in a learning

mode and the consultant in a teaching mode.

4. The *developer*: this consultant is mainly occupied with developing the client or client organization from within. The consultant's contribution may be to open new perspectives on the problem, to point out alternative ways of thinking, or simply to ask naïve questions, listen closely and observe while the client works on his own problems. Again, the consultant and the client work in close collaboration, and the consultant may adopt either a symmetrical or a complementary stance.

Clearly, in each of these roles the contribution of the consultant is different. As an expert, the consultant provides knowledge and solutions, as a process manager the consultant provides pace and progress. In the other two roles, the focus is much more on the learning achieved by the client and on increasing the capacity of the client to do things differently. As a trainer, the consultant provides new challenges and approaches, as a developer the consultant offers new perspectives and questions. In these two roles, therefore, the consultant contributes more to the conditions for new action and learning rather than being himself responsible for new actions or new learning.

However, there are also similarities in the contributions of different consultants in this implementation phase. Most consultants, whatever their role in the consulting assignment, will reflect back the information and ideas that they have assembled in the preceding exploration phase. In view of the subjectivity of this process of feeding back information and impressions, the consultant will often relate his or her own feelings and experiences. Much of the feedback may touch sensitive spots in the client's approach to the problem: the expert may tell the client that he has been doing something wrong, and show how to do it better; the process manager may try to bring the client closer to the "unfinished business" and urge the client to move on; the trainer may offer challenging experiences, and the developer may offer challenging perspectives. In *King Lear*, all advisers are geared towards the king's development, and all remain fairly close to the role of developer.

What I believe to be most vital for consultants in this stage of consulting is to be conscious of one's own role and contribution. Therefore, I view consulting in this stage to be crucially "self-monitoring" and "self-directing". It is all about having the capacity, first, to observe oneself in interaction, and second, when necessary, to have other options at one's disposal within this interaction. Generally, the client's full attention is taken by his own problems and fortunes. The consultant, on the contrary, should maintain enough distance and space to reflect on and monitor the situation, and to choose consciously a variety of interventions.

Self-monitoring and self-directing provides a deeper way of looking at the consultant's contribution, precisely because they encompass both role and intervention. Therefore, at this stage of the assignment, the consultant may consciously decide, as a result of self-monitoring, to "step out of role" and to contribute in a way different to the one originally contracted. If so, the consultant needs to be careful and should be conscious that he is covertly renegotiating the contract at a very sensitive moment, which may lead to quite well-founded "resistance" from the client.

The following are some aspects of consulting that will be considered in this chapter:

- the "crisis" and "peripeteia" of making a difference: the consultant's judgement and the upset this judgement may cause;
- is being symmetrical and supportive enough, or does a consultant also need to be complementary and challenging;
- the testing of the client–consultant relationship;
- resistance to change and where it may come from.

b. King Lear (III.1–III.7)

King Lear's major crisis occurs in the famous scene on the heath. As the Earl of Kent starts his search for the king at an ungodly hour, he hears from a passer-by that Lear, in his impotent anger, contends with the elements and demands from them that they return to their primordial state. Lear roams the heath, accompanied by his Fool, screaming at the wind and rain:

> [...] here I stand, your slave,
> A poor, infirm, weak and despised old man,
> But yet I call you servile ministers. [III.2.19]

The minute Kent finds Lear, he tries to give him shelter in a hovel on the heath. To their astonishment they find the hovel occupied by a pitiful creature who calls himself Poor Tom (Edgar). His gibberish, in which he claims to be pursued by *the foul fiend* and other demons, has a curious appeal to the weakened king: Lear straightaway tears off all his clothes so as to become like Poor Tom. At that point, the Earl of Gloucester enters the scene, a man full of compassion. He invites the entire company to spend the night in a house near the castle. It takes a great deal of persuasion, and the inclusion of Poor Tom, to get King Lear to go to the house. Inside, the crisis comes to a head in a terzetto of insane lyricism: the Fool reflecting, Edgar exorcizing demons and Lear, the only one who has really lost his bearings, gnawed by remorse and grief, trying to cope with the unbearable pain that Goneril and Regan have caused him. Lear's mind has now completely sunk into fantasies: the hell where his daughters are shrieking, a court of law where they are tried and, when he gets exhausted, his old luxurious bedroom in the palace. His flights of imagination are sometimes so shocking that even Edgar gets emotional, forgetting his role and losing his childish tone. After Gloucester lets Lear escape to Dover, together with Kent and the Fool, Edgar delivers a final reflective speech:

> How light and portable my pain seems now,
> When that which makes me bend makes the King bow,
> He childed as I fathered. [III.6.105]

Gloucester has to deal with another set of problems when the vicious Edmund plays the same trick on him as he did on Edgar, by sending the Duke of Cornwall a confidential letter accusing Gloucester of treachery. This results in the tragedy's first confrontation with physical cruelty: Cornwall and Regan cut out Gloucester's eyes. A servant takes Gloucester's side and fatally wounds Cornwall. Ironically, at the very moment he becomes blind, Gloucester realizes that it was Edmund who betrayed both Edgar and himself.

c. The session on the heath

In the middle of his crisis, King Lear has retreated to the heath accompanied by three valuable advisers. However, he does not put their sharp insights into practice as yet, because in contrast to his advisers' interpretations, Lear's own interpretation of the events puts the emphasis on (1) the fact that he has done nothing wrong: ... *I am a man / More sinned against than sinning* (III.2.59), and (2) the conclusion that he has apparently put too much trust in his daughters: he gave them all he had assuming that he would be well taken care of in his old age.

All three advisers touch a spot that is still too sensitive for Lear: the giving away of his kingdom and thereby the abdication of his responsibilities. However, as we shall see, the advice he is given does have an effect, but not until the fourth Act in which Lear repents his deeds and undergoes a fundamental transformation.

It is obvious that Lear is most taken by his recently found, third adviser. The philosophical approach, as Lear calls it, of Poor Tom (really Edgar in disguise) carries an extraordinary appeal.

Edgar seems to strike up a friendship with the demons that beset him and plays with them like a child. Similarly, he addresses Lear in a playful, childlike tone. Lear explicitly seeks out Edgar as his adviser: *I will keep still with my philosopher* (III.4.173). This phrase exemplifies Lear's style and personality: he asks for his philosopher; he wants his advice and yet, once he has it, he wants to keep still, passive, and retreat from the world.

Lear's three advisers are reminiscent of the three personalities that we all have within us, according to the theory of Transactional Analysis (Berne, 1964): the parent, the adult, and the child. The Fool is clearly superior to, and wiser than, the king, yet he challenges his Nuncle Lear to an exciting symmetrical parent–parent relationship. Lear accepts this relationship, but he cannot refrain from addressing the Fool with the words *"my boy"*, thereby stressing the difference in status between a king and a Fool. Moreover, it appears as if Lear pays no attention at all to the advice the Fool gives him. This in spite of the fact that the Fool proves with everything he says that he has great insight into Lear's problems and their origins. Lear only occasionally adopts the surrealistic tone and images the Fool uses, especially in the final stages of his madness.

Kent is the adult who, time and again, asks Lear in very clear terms to behave like an adult. Kent receives replies that are equally clear, for instance at the time of his expulsion or later, when he is accepted as Lear's servant. However, Lear is not the kind of king to stay in the adult role for long, and he pays little heed to the sound, practical advice his Earl, and servant, gives him.

Poor Tom is the self-proclaimed child: "if I stand no chance at all, I might as well act crazy" is what Edgar, like Hamlet, must have thought. When Lear meets him, he is a strange, creative boy who claims to be pursued by demons. And Lear loves to be like an irresponsible child, resulting in a third acceptance of a symmetrical relationship with an adviser (child–child in this case). Moreover, in Edgar's stories, which are marked by childlike fear and childlike happiness, Lear finds something that can actually help him in his crisis, something that he is willing to listen to, because it suits his character. It fits his longing for renunciation, and hence his ill fated decrees in the first Act. This "something", this new, "philosophical" view is the acceptance of his sombre destiny. Edgar both accepts his misery and puts it into perspective; he later calls himself: *A most poor man, made tame to fortune's blows* (IV.6.218). From the moment he meets Edgar, Lear is much better able to accept things as they are.

d. The implementation phase

The moment at which the transition from gathering information to taking action is effectuated, can never be exactly determined. The very presence in an organization of a consultant who is gathering information is in itself a very conspicuous change. Still, there is another turning point in the process, which occurs when his information is presented. That presentation is no more objective than the information itself. The idea is to present a new point of view to the client organization—either together with the person representing the client or on your own—and to engage other people's interest. An essential factor that determines the success of the consulting process is the *relationship* that the client and the consultant have built up. In the implementation phase, this relationship is tested for the first time.

Where is the drama in this phase?

In dramaturgy, this phase is described as that of crisis and peripeteia, or literally of "judgement" and "upset". The *upset* is the protagonist's reversal of fortune, with, simultaneously or directly following, a fundamental shift in point of view, priorities and approach; something which in the consulting literature is called a transformational change (see also Tichy & Devanna, 1986).

The upset occurs at the culmination or highest point of the tension curve of the drama—which is the dramaturgical meaning of crisis!—usually heralded by means of a *judgement*, which is an independent personal reflection on the situation of the protagonist. In Greek tragedies, this is often a divine judgement. In *King Lear*, the judgement consists of the collective statements of the three advisers. The same thing happens in the management consulting process: in this phase, the consultant presents a well-founded, personal analysis of the situation, which the client rightly receives as an independent judgment. In consulting, the judgement of the consultant often proves to reflect an already existing "inner voice" of the client.

Now the client (organization) is invited to look at the situation from a different perspective or even to do things differently in the future. The consultant actually intervenes in the situation, making this phase the one in which *resistance* to change can surface. Resistance can take many forms: such as doubt and insecurity, open hostility, or even exaggerated approval of the new perspectives and suggestions. The forms resistance takes may appear as "dramatic": strong emotions can be involved. That should not surprise us when we realize that the source of such resistance is also a dramatic one: the core of a living system, person, or organization, a system that is characterized by an inherent drive for self-preservation, is invited to become "different". This means that the system is requested to abstain temporarily and in part from one of its most essential functions. As what is to replace the old does not yet exist, the advice will initially cause great insecurity and anxiety, often expressed as resistance. The art is to get to the next phase, in which change is generated from within and thus supports itself.

It is interesting to examine just where resistance comes from. To start with, the client often asks who or what is to blame for the undesired situation. The consultant will attempt to transform the question of blame, which is counterproductive, into a question of responsibilities. Moreover, he will encourage the client to consider future responsibilities, rather than looking back. The consultant may ask, for example: "What division of tasks and responsibilities might lead to the necessary improvements?" If the consultant defends his proposals for the future empathically and compellingly, it is possible that he will encounter opposition from the client (organization). Force is a justifiable ground for resistance (Putnam, 1979). That means that the client is not responsible for all resistance that occurs: the consultant also has responsibility in this respect. A salient detail in *King Lear* is that the very competent advisers the king has at his disposal *do not offer advice* in this phase of the play (Kent does offer advice in the first Act and is expelled immediately: an action on Lear's part that may well be described as resistance). They only offer new, appealing analyses of the problem that are so strong that the King cannot but consider them. Often in this phase, a bold, well-chosen judgement is enough to initiate a change for the better. Moreover, once the client acquires a new perspective on the situation, he is himself the foremost expert when it comes to solutions (Block, 1981).

To be able to deal with the tensions occurring in this phase in particular, a solid relationship between the client and the consultant, and agreement about the nature of this relationship, are of crucial importance. As we can see in *King Lear*, a symmetrical relationship, whatever its precise nature, is to be preferred. In such a relationship, both parties are aware of their shared responsibility. Moreover, the rivalry and creativity the relationship invites can be put to good use. In this sense, Edgar shows himself to be a skilled adviser. He shares experiences similar to those of his client, he has an original point of view, and he shows sincere compassion and patience in demonstrating, rather than imposing, a different attitude to life.

CHAPTER FOUR

Denouement

a. Consulting: key issues in making it last

In the fourth phase of consulting, the phase of the denouement or resolution, the consultant's aim is mainly to facilitate what is now working. In a successful assignment, the consultant can now lean back a little, do more self-monitoring without too much self-directing, and try to stay with whatever the client's development is. The consultant becomes gradually more like a member of the audience in a theatre: observing, perhaps identifying with, and pondering on what takes place on the central stage. For the client and the client organization, there may still be a lot of uncertainty, threat, unexpected turns of events, and ambiguity towards the consultant's interventions. If the interventions are working well, however, these anxieties may diminish and even dissolve with time.

If the assignment has progressed well enough to develop into this phase in the first place, the consultant now has the opportunity to witness change from close quarters. Whether or not he has had a share in producing the change, somewhere a difference has been created in the client's fortunes. This difference may initially be very small, fragile, or fluctuating, thus not fully and continuously present. Such is the case in many of the characters experiencing change in the tragedy *King Lear*. Or it may be full and total, such as we have seen in the change from Edgar to Poor Tom, or such as we will see presently in the new position of the Duke of Albany. However the onset of the change occurs, many consultants feel privileged to witness it and to nourish it with further consulting interventions. The essence of these nourishing interventions is to support the change, to remain mindful and aware of its nature and progression, and to facilitate its growth regardless of regular occurrences of insecurity, relapse, and weakening.

Mirroring the relapses and temptations that the client and the client organization may experience, the consultant may feel many temptations in this phase. One temptation is to try to continue "making a difference", explaining again and again the great plan and the way to proceed. This temptation is counterproductive if the consultant continues intervening when the client is already capable of implementing the change himself. Another temptation is to leave too early and to move on to seemingly more "interesting" and more "dramatic" assignments, when the current assignment is still in need of supportive interventions from the consultant.

There is still a lot for the consultant to do, if only to encourage the change that is taking place and to encourage the consolidation of whatever has started. Moreover, the subtle art of "letting go" begins in this phase, where the consultant tries to move gently away from the centre of the action.

The following are some aspects of consulting that will be considered in this chapter:

- the thrill and excitement of seeing new forms of behaviour and commitment to change;
- the art of dealing with ambiguity and relapses;
- the challenge of remaining equally present and involved even if the assignment becomes less exciting;
- the dangers of becoming mutually dependent.

b. King Lear (IV.1–IV.7)

The fourth Act of *King Lear*, much more so than the other Acts, is full of unexpected turns of events and fundamental changes in the characters. The entire act is permeated by the threat of war: the King of France and Cordelia have landed in Dover, and Goneril and Regan are in their castles preparing for battle. Edmund, whose star is rising rapidly, joins them in their preparation. After the mutilation and disappearance of Gloucester, Edmund himself becomes the Earl of Gloucester. In addition Edmund has won the hearts of both Regan and Goneril. They are therefore pitted not only against France, but also against each other. Oswald, the lackey, carries to Edmund fiery letters from both sisters. As for their legal husbands, the Duke of Cornwall dies of the wound inflicted by the servant, and the Duke of Albany gets into a conflict with his wife Goneril because he is unexpectedly and fiercely opposed to the way she treated her father. However, Albany remains willing to act against the foreign invader, France.

Edgar sees his father approach on the heath, accompanied by an old servant. They do not recognize Edgar, but Gloucester does ask Poor Tom to take him to Dover. This forces Edgar to remain in his role of Poor Tom, however difficult this is for him in the circumstances. Gloucester has grown world-weary: all he wants is to go to Dover so he may jump off a cliff and end his life. Upon their arrival in Dover, Edgar tries to dissuade him from this idea one step at a time. First he fools Gloucester by telling him that they are on top of a cliff, and all he has to do is jump. Gloucester says farewell to life and falls headlong on the ground. Next, Edgar adopts a new role, that of a fisherman who finds Gloucester after he has "miraculously" survived his great fall. He also starts calling Gloucester father, but this goes unnoticed. Suddenly Oswald appears, who wants to kill Gloucester because Regan has put a price on his head. Edgar intervenes, kills Oswald, and on his body he finds a highly compromising letter from Goneril to Edmund in which she asks him to kill her husband Albany after the battle.

Cordelia arrives in Dover, full of compassion and concern, accompanied by a doctor who will cure King Lear of his insanity. Lear, who suddenly appears with a crown of wild flowers on his head, calls himself once again *every inch a King* (IV.6.107), yet continues to speak in brilliant associative madness, in which each word calls forth the next. Nevertheless, Lear has gained in self-awareness, as demonstrated by fragments of his speech:

Thou knowst the first time that we smell the air
We waul and cry. [IV.6.175]

and

> I am even
> The natural fool of fortune. [IV.6.186]

He was born to let his fate be determined by others! His grumbling about the evil of the world also illustrates his new insight: *They flattered me like a dog* (IV.6.96). Lear has no desire anymore to direct the course of events, and he unleashes his wild associations on all new events as they occur. He has learned to adopt the "philosophical attitude" that he so admired in Poor Tom. For example, Lear imagines his two eldest daughters being brought to justice, but when someone suddenly puts a hand on his shoulder, he imagines himself in the dock: he offers no resistance and turns it into a game, simulating his escape.

The king is made to sleep by the doctor, and when Cordelia kisses him he wakes up, a severely weakened man. Immediately after he recognizes Cordelia, he drops to his knees and begs her forgiveness in a new tone of voice: soft, warm, and fatherly:

> Pray do not mock me.
> I am a very foolish, fond old man [IV.7.59].

This is an extraordinarily touching scene.

c. Catharsis

Aristotle (4th century BC) used the word catharsis—purification—to describe what the audience, in the grips of pity and terror, goes through in this phase of the drama. Later, catharsis was also used to characterize the fundamental transformation of the protagonist in many tragedies. In the fourth Act of *King Lear*, not only does the king learn from his downfall, but almost all characters find themselves profoundly changed, with varying outcomes. A kind of "parting of the ways" takes place: on the one side those who persevere in their ruthless conceit and quickly become perverse: Goneril, Regan, Edmund, and Oswald; and on the other side those who are honestly trying to find a way out of this suffocating tragedy: Lear, Gloucester, and Albany. The other characters either do not undergo major changes or, like Edgar, learned their lesson in the first Act.

For Lear and Gloucester, the main theme remains "responsibility".

Gloucester thought he could take responsibility, that his world was relatively simple with a good son (Edmund) and a bad son (Edgar) and that, after Lear's resignation, he could serve the new powers in good faith. However, as we have witnessed, this view of the world was shaken to its very foundations and Gloucester himself turned out not to be immune: blind and without a title, he is left to roam the earth. It is striking with what determination Gloucester refuses to make use of his remaining options: offering support to King Lear and Cordelia, or searching for his disowned son Edgar and begging his forgiveness. Instead, Gloucester wants nothing more than to die. In the composition of the drama, Gloucester's death-wish mirrors and expands on Lear's approach, because it pursues the theme of abdicating responsibilities to the extreme.

As for King Lear: the development of his madness is one of Shakespeare's great achievements in this tragedy. Lear's madness is his ultimate flight from responsibility. Lear gradually becomes completely irresponsible, in both his actions and his words. It is, therefore, worthwhile to take a closer look at the way his madness is built up, step by step, and to follow it in Lear's own words:

1. The first signs are visible in the very first Act, after Goneril's affront. In I.5.42 Lear cries out

   O, let me not be mad, not mad, sweet heaven!
   Keep me in temper. I would not be mad!

   This shows that, given his unrestrained outbursts of anger, he already regards madness as a possible outcome.
2. In Act II, after Regan's affront, it is as if the ground melts from under Lear's feet. He has expelled one daughter from his kingdom and the other two show themselves to be highly unreliable, hostile creatures. Lear's words are full of hints at his madness. He seems to want to call insanity down upon himself and uses it to put pressure on others, as in II.4.216: *I prithee, daughter, do not make me mad.* His words become staccato; he constantly seeks a new path of escape. His last words to Regan and Goneril are:

   You think I'll weep.
   No, I'll not weep. I have full cause of weeping,
   But this heart shall break into a hundred thousand flaws
   Or ere I'll weep—O Fool, I shall go mad! [II.4.280]

In Lear's view there are only two alternatives (to weep or to go mad), neither of which is meant to intervene in the situation, but rather to soften the pain via the roundabout route of evoking the pity of others.

3. In the beginning of the third Act, Lear appears to be a wrathful man whose words make the world tremble. However, by exhausting himself like this, he opens the doors to madness even further, and he knows it: *My wits begin to turn* (III.2.67). He claims not to feel the wind and the rain, because

> [...] This tempest in my mind
> Doth from my senses take all feeling else
> Save what beats there. [III.4.12]

Again, to him the only alternatives are to weep or to go mad.

4. The meeting with Poor Tom marks a new phase. Lear bombards this pitiful, incoherently talking creature with questions. From the very start, Lear identifies with Edgar, and he asks time and again if Poor Tom also has daughters who have driven him to this state. By ripping off his clothes, Lear loses touch with surrounding reality. He lets himself be led by his inner turmoil rather than by somebody else's influence.

5. Next, in the house near the castle, he is lost in his own fantasy world. His words are filled with images, bursts of revenge, cries of victory, spells of intoxication, and bouts of ecstasy. Lost in his fantasies, Lear disappears from the stage for over six scenes.

6. When Lear returns in IV.6.80 we can tell he has changed little: one image still calls forth another and Lear has completely disappeared into his own world. Edgar's reaction when he sees Lear is to cry out: *O thou side-piercing sight!* (IV.6.85). Lear's reply illustrates his madness better than any description could:

> Nature's above art in that respect. There's your press-money.
> That fellow handles his bow like a crowkeeper.
> Draw me a clothier's yard.
> Look, look, a mouse!
> Peace, peace! This piece of toasted cheese will do't.
> There's my gauntlet. I'll prove it on a giant.
> Bring up the brown bills.
> O, well flown, bird, i'th clout, i'th clout! Whew!
> Give the word. [IV.6.86]

Still, as Edgar realizes, there is *reason in madness* (IV.6.173) and Lear's reflections show that he is now less involved and less focused on himself than he was earlier.

7. With a madness such as King Lear experiences, there is little to be done, except to make him sleep, which is done off stage. When Lear wakes up, he is still very drowsy but able to communicate coherently.

Summarizing, we may conclude that the turning point in Lear's illness coincides with his meeting Edgar, after which a process of change commences. What Edgar means to Lear's development cannot be overestimated: in the first place, he is apparently in as bad a state as Lear, if indeed not in a worse one. Recognizing this, Lear trusts him immediately, just as he had earlier trusted the Fool. Neither represents a position of power and neither wants anything from him. In the second place, Edgar shows Lear how, even under extreme circumstances, composure and perseverance are possible by first and foremost accepting your destiny. Finally, in Edgar's monologues, we find that he more than anybody is touched by the King's sad fate; Edgar is an adviser with great compassion. Once Lear learns to accept his fate, he seizes responsibility for his own life once again, even though it remains impossible for him to take true responsibility for others.

d. The consolidation phase

In this phase, an organization starts to function in a truly different way; the initiative of the client and the involvement of the consultant have achieved an effect. Because of the autonomous nature of the changes it is necessary to pay undiminished attention to them. There is always a danger that the advice will only give the appearance of being anchored or institutionalized, and that in reality the situation will be drawn back to the old state unnoticed ("One swallow does not make a summer"). At the same time, the consultant tries to make himself dispensable, because he knows the assignment will have to be concluded by his departure.

Where is the drama in this phase?

The moment of truth is upon us: it is clear to everyone that something has to happen and that the consultant has proposed something new. But it remains a matter of choice. Roughly speaking, there are now three possibilities.

1. The client persists with his own traditional approach. In this case he will be less and less open to the consultant and will possibly become inflexible or uninterested. We see this clearly depicted in *King Lear* in the character of Gloucester, who in the end wants nothing but to die and cannot be dissuaded from this idea by any means. This leaves the consultant with no other options than to quickly move on to the final phase, that of evaluation and departure.

2. The client discovers a new approach on his own, independent of the consultant. Now it depends on the circumstances whether or not the consultant can still contribute to the process. The fact that the client has been successful in finding a new approach generally increases the chances of success: the client has taken full responsibility. It is up to the consultant to forget his own vanity and not to be carried away by feelings of being unappreciated. He can gain satisfaction from the fact that an assignment has been successfully completed, by whatever means.

3. The advice is received with enthusiasm and is implemented. The consultant is now often invited to support the client during the consolidation of the changes. He happily does this and is willing to elaborate on his proposals from the previous phase or adjust them to meet the requirements of specific problems. A danger lurks in this gratifying development, however. A mutual dependency of client and consultant may result: the consultant needs the client for his success story and the client needs the consultant in order to be able to carry on in the new situation.

Whatever relationship or division of tasks occurs in this phase, two features are typical: in the first place, the client becomes increasingly independent and autonomous. This happens to most characters in *King Lear* also: they try to exert less influence on each other (apart from Edgar's failed attempts with his father, Gloucester). The other feature is the fact that for the consultant, during this phase the final phase, that of evaluation and completion, already looms. Therefore, the responsibility of consultant and client in this phase is true commitment to each other, without undertaking to do something the other is capable of doing for himself.

CHAPTER FIVE

Catastrophe and exodus

a. Consulting: key issues in letting go

I n the fifth and final phase of consulting, the consultant's aim is mainly to end the consulting relationship in such a way that it can be rekindled whenever required. He is focused on letting go and stepping out of the client organization, albeit in a way that does not preclude stepping back in, nor prevent further strengthening of the ongoing manifestation of the assignment's effects.

In the theatre the boundaries are clear. We know when the play is over, if only from the change in light or the clapping of the audience. We have not allowed the protagonists to really become part of our life; we can walk out of the theatre and leave the whole plot behind us. Not so in consulting. In consulting, there is a strong investment by both client and consultant in the consulting relationship, and there are good reasons for continuing this relationship at every moment: the client keeps the luxury of an outsider who is knowledgeable and involved, and the consultant has the benefit of rewards and the feeling that he is of service. So the consultant and the client can easily become mutually dependent on one another for their success and their survival.

It is important, therefore, for both client and consultant to let go and move on to more autonomous positions. Consulting is temporary and bounded by clear limits of effectiveness, which can extend from a few hours to a few years. Unless a complete redefining and re-contracting takes place, a consultant who stays on for more than "enough time" is usually there to the detriment of both client and consultant, or at the very least experiences a change in role from consultant to manager.

A strong case for "letting go", in order not to become mutually dependent with the client, has been made by Roger Harrison. In his article on organizations' addictions to consultants and consultants' co-dependency with organizations, he suggests six powerful requirements for consultants who want to go through this phase of "exodus" healthily (Harrison, 1997):

1. First and foremost, the consultant practices detachment. He lets go of worry about situations in the client organization and he does not attempt to control what happens there. He abandons any personal mission to teach the client to live better. He does not depend on his clients emotionally or financially.
2. The consultant approaches his client with integrity and with compassion, neither proselytizing for his own version of the truth, nor distorting his truth to make it more palatable to his client.
3. The consultant lets go of responsibility for any harm that his client organization may do in the world, and for undoing or preventing it, except through speaking his mind. Neither does he take credit for the good they do, nor for the progress they make.
4. The consultant acknowledges his own faults, inadequacies and betrayals to himself and to others, and to the best of his ability forgives those of his clients.
5. The consultant seeks to experience to the full any sorrow and despair which he feels over what is going on in the client's organization, so that he can become free of the apathy, powerlessness and emotional deadness that attend the suppression of these feelings.
6. While accepting the disturbing knowledge that many things are in a mess and he cannot fix all of them, the consultant

continues, with or without hope, to act in ways he believes are constructive.

Supporting these quite solemn requirements, some more mundane but nevertheless helpful practices can be adopted in this last stage of the consulting process, such as looking back and evaluating the assignment in order to extract and formulate learning that can help with different but similar future assignments, and celebrating and proclaiming the end of the intervention, inside or outside the client organization.

The following are some aspects of consulting that will be considered in this chapter:

- the paradox of change, where an individual can change to the core and still remain the same;
- the beautiful discovery by the consultant that his client has become a calm rock in a sea of stormy waters, which is a sign of profound and lasting change;
- it being no one else but the client who takes the praise and the blame for the outcome of the consulting assignment;
- surviving the assignment and making amendments, in order to be ready for the next;
- the final survey of checks and balances that will keep the consolidated change in place;
- evaluation of the consulting assignment in terms of changes to the client, his role and his organization.

b. King Lear (V.1–V.3)

Just before the battle, the Duke of Albany's camp is permeated by mutual distrust: Edmund and Regan do not trust Albany's cooperation, Regan does not believe in Edmund's loyalty to her, and Regan and Goneril communicate in an icy manner. When the armies go to battle, Edgar suddenly appears, takes Albany aside, shows him Goneril's letter to Edmund in which she plots on Albany's life, and disappears again. Independently, in a brief monologue, Edmund reveals himself again to be a self-serving and ruthlessly calculating schemer.

The battle itself takes place off stage and is over in no time: in a scene of a mere eleven lines that for me captures the essence of the entire play, we are shown, from the position of Edgar and Gloucester, how King Lear has to accept his defeat. Edmund arrests Lear and Cordelia and sends them to the dungeon. There, Lear cares for and consoles his daughter:

> [...] so we'll live,
> And pray, and sing, and tell old tales, and laugh
> At gilded butterflies [V.3.11]

Edmund secretly orders his captain to kill them, after which Albany appears, but he is too late to claim the prisoners.

When Regan calls Edmund "hers" under Goneril's jealous eyes, Albany issues a warrant against Edmund, accusing him of high treason. To the horror of the two sisters he then throws his gauntlet at Edmund's feet. Regan suddenly feels unwell, which, it becomes clear, is the result of Goneril having poisoned her. Albany sounds the trumpet, summoning everyone to file complaints against Edmund. Then Edgar appears, still disguised, takes on his half-brother in single combat, and wins, mortally wounding Edmund. Albany makes sure Edgar does not kill Edmund immediately, so that he can confront the latter publicly with the compromising letter from Goneril. Goneril, beside herself with rage, disappears and kills herself. Edmund confesses to his crimes. Edgar now makes himself known. He also brings the news of the death of Gloucester, whose heart broke when Edgar revealed his identity to him.

When the bodies of Goneril and Regan are brought in, Edmund is so shaken that he reveals his plot against Lear and Cordelia. The officer sent to prevent further misery arrives too late: Cordelia died on the gallows. Lear enters the stage carrying his dead, beloved daughter in his arms. After an outburst of grief, he dies too. Finally he is ready and "grown wise before he grew old". Lear's last words are full of ambiguity and a sense of being overwhelmed, as they break into trancelike repetition, from *No, no, no life!* (5.3.304) to *Never, never, never, never, never* (5.3.307) and on to *O, o, o, o* (5.3.308), and finally to:

> [...] Look on her.
> Look, her lips.
> Look there, look there! [5.3.309]

Clearly, he dies with all his attention fully focused on Cordelia.

Edmund dies as well. Albany's reaction to the event is a cool one: *That's but a trifle here* (V.3. 294). Thus, after King Lear's death, there are only three men left: Albany, Kent and Edgar. And they allow Edgar to reign the kingdom and have the last word:

The weight of this sad time we must obey;
Speak what we feel, not what we ought to say.
The oldest hath borne most. We that are young
Shall never see so much, nor live so long [V.3.321]

c. Saevis tranquillus in undis

At the beginning of the fifth Act, the dramatic transformation process has already been completed; the main characters have learned what they had to learn, and now the fate of all is quickly sealed. All the crises, all the violence and misery that have engulfed the protagonists and the state of England are quickly concluded and all that is left is for the more contemplative characters to present a final evaluation.

In the fifth Act, King Lear proves to have changed and yet remained himself. He now radiates great calm, strength, and decisiveness, at a time when the world has become an explosive and violent battlefield. He is a paragon of calm in the middle of stormy waters: *"saevis tranquillus in undis"* (the motto of the Dutch *pater patriae*, William the Silent). In addition, Lear has become a warm and loving father to Cordelia, speaking with encouraging and heartening words when she receives further bad news. But at the same time, King Lear has remained himself. He has retained his trait of extreme renunciation and his desire to lead a secluded life. When Edmund sends him to prison, Lear's reaction is almost jubilant:

[...] Come, let's away to prison.
We two alone will sing like birds i' th' cage. [V.3.8]

Shakespeare has given us a masterful portrayal of the change paradox (Selvini Palazzoli *et al.*, 1975) of the consulting process in this *King Lear*: how a person can change to the core, and still remain the same person!

At the end of the play, we are left with three people who deserve to survive, even though we would have liked King Lear, Gloucester, and Cordelia to survive as well. They were too much involved in the tragedy to survive, however. We have not heard of the Fool since Act III. It is more likely that Lear is referring to his daughter than to him when he says in V.3.304: *And my poor fool is hanged!*

Why would these three men survive? The Duke of Albany mended his ways and played a heroic part by beating the French while remaining loyal to his king. Kent remains above all the conscientious adviser: he has made himself heard from the very start, but we cannot expect of him that he get overly caught up in the developments. However, he foresees an early death, now that he is without his king:

I have a journey, sir, shortly to go.
My master calls me; I must not say no. [V.3.319]

Edgar, the true hero of this drama, has done his utmost and, in spite of all his hardships, has never missed a chance to intervene in a constructive way. It is appropriate that he speaks the final words, an honour usually given to an old and wise character.

d. The evaluation phase

In this phase, the consultant checks once again, in cooperation with the client, whether there are sufficient measures in place to guarantee the consolidation of the change. If this is not the case, they go back to the previous phase, so that measures may be reinforced. If the change has indeed been "institutionalized" they can take stock. In this final evaluation, the entire project is examined once again, as well as the extent to which the project has met the expectations laid down under the terms of the contract. Unexpected events and changed objectives that occurred during the project, as well as current quality requirements, can be considered in the process. Once the evaluation is completed, the project may be concluded.

Where is the drama in this phase?

At the beginning of this phase, the drama proper is over: the die has been cast, the client organization has made its choice. If things have gone well, the client organization now draws on its own new and unexpected reserves and calmly stays on course in the turbulent waters that surround it. The client monitors the changes and can begin to reap the benefits. Difficulties can arise only if it is not understood that the benefits and rewards belong to the client and to the client alone. The danger of too large a degree of mutual dependence is present in this phase. On the one hand: who would want to end a successful consulting process? The relationship is good, the parties have achieved a great deal together, and they are content. On the other hand: if things do not go as expected, it is understandable that the consultant will be blamed. Subsequently, he will be summoned in again, and will be put to work until the expectations are met. In both cases, the danger of a useless continuation of consultations between client and consultant looms large. In this phase the consultant, who may be tempted to stay, is responsible for concluding the project, however superfluous that may seem.

A thorough final evaluation may facilitate the process of disengagement: expectations and risks are listed one more time, and the evaluation provides the client with a document with which he himself can monitor the ongoing change.

As an evaluation of the consulting process in *King Lear*, I would like to offer the following.

The responsibility of the management consultant has earlier been described as working together with the client to improve the client's fortunes. With regard to that responsibility, we can distinguish three aspects: responsibility for the person of the client, responsibility for the role of the client, and responsibility for the organization of the client. To what extent have the consultants in *King Lear* accomplished their goal?

Person: Due to unfortunate circumstances and more specifically, due to Edmund's final intrigue, King Lear dies at the end of the play. However, if we disregard Lear's death, we can describe the process relating to the person of King Lear as very successful. Lear has become both more truly himself and more effective in terms of coping with his circumstances.

Role: Most changes occur with respect to role, as Lear moves from being king, retired king, "nothing", patient, and warrior, to prisoner-of-war. In the very first scene of the play, Lear loses his role as king, so for a consultant little can be achieved there. In the fifth Act, however, he fulfils his roles of father and elderly statesman perfectly.

Organization: It seems plausible that England will flourish under Edgar's rule. This means that when the blood on the battlefield has dried, the consulting process has been successfully completed in this regard also.

These favourable outcomes aside, the consulting process in *King Lear* is marked above all by violence and death. These do not personally affect Lear's advisers, however: they are left behind, relatively unharmed and alone, ready to move on to their next assignments.

Conclusion

The tragedy is over. The events were gripping, bloody and intensely sad. We are left with a sense of emptiness, anxiety and compassion, but also with the realization that we have been observing something true, a story from which we can learn. In this conclusion, I will briefly summarize once again what we have learned from *King Lear* in the preceding pages.

First, we need to distinguish between two different levels of the drama, the level of "what *King Lear* is" and the level of "what *King Lear* is about":

On the one hand, *King Lear* "is" a tragedy, an ill-fated process of cleansing. It is also a process which permits us to learn from a problematic situation. In this respect *King Lear* can be seen as a consulting process. This is also illustrated by the similarity between the phases of a classical tragedy and those of a consulting process, the five "acts". However, the presence of the three main characters bearing the role of adviser and the development of the protagonist are the main indicators of a consulting process. As we have seen, the consulting process in *King Lear* is eminently successful: in the last Act, the old king is able to understand, accept and improve his situation. In this regard, the tragedy *King Lear* shows us how it should be done.

On the other hand, *King Lear* "is about" the theme of taking responsibility for one's own situation. Lear's first actions in the play, in which the king abdicates completely his own responsibilities, prove to be fatal to him, to his country, and to his daughters. In line with the conventions of classical tragedy, fate does not have mercy on the failing protagonist. In this respect, *King Lear* is everything but a success story. Abdicating one's responsibilities is a very relevant issue in relation to the consulting process, because in that process responsibilities must be assumed and shared with care by the consultant and the client. In that respect, King Lear's personal tragedy demonstrates how it should not be done.

As an attentive audience watching the tragedy unfold, we have learned on both levels. That should not surprise us, because responsibility is one of the cornerstones of a successful consulting process (Block, 1981). As a drama, *King Lear* provides a fresh look at the consulting process while at the same time, in the reflections of the main characters, giving us ample opportunity to explore the theme of responsibility. For the manager and the management consultant, the most important thing *King Lear* has to offer can be formulated as the reverse of King Lear's maxim expressed in I.1.89: *Nothing will come of nothing*, and I.4.130: *Nothing can be made out of nothing*. The reverse would be: *something can come of nothing*. This slightly cryptic phrase can be applied to three approaches used by consultants. These are discussed below, using examples taken from the play.

1. Up by way of down

All too often we find that there is, in fact, a great deal to be gained from an apparently hopeless situation, but only once we accept it by literally choosing to be "be-littled". King Lear is belittled to an extreme, and the Fool rubs it in:

> Thou wast a pretty fellow when thou hadst no need to care for her frowning. Now thou art an O without a figure. I am better than thou art, now. I am a fool; thou art nothing. [I.4.188]

In the course of the play, Lear moves from being King of England to being a pitiful beggar who cannot even get his thoughts straight. And from the moment he accepts that, in the fourth Act (*They told me I was everything; 'tis a lie, I am not ague-proof* [IV.6.104]), things start improving and he can revert to feeling *every inch a king* (IV.6.107). Another example can be found in Edgar, whose hardships in the second Act equal those of Lear. Edgar immediately chooses his belittling and turns himself into a beggar, saying *That's something yet. Edgar, I nothing am* (II.3.21). In this way he is from the start able to understand and accept his circumstances, which are just as dire as those of the king. The only things he can reproach himself for are being too naïve and too trusting. From that moment, matured by his experience, he is even able to take upon himself the role of adviser to others.

In the consulting process too, the initial outlook is frequently bleak. It is sometimes necessary for the client to "get up by going down" (see also Leary, 1957). In other words: to choose for one's own limitations or loss, and thus create a situation in which one can get a handle on the future. That also relates directly to responsibility. In the initial situation, the difficulties are *symptoms* (a Greek word which literally means "mishaps") that get the better of the client. By consciously choosing to accept a difficult situation, the client takes responsibility for it and thereby acquires a starting point from which he or she can work to change it. Kent aptly expresses the rewards of such a choice. When he is put in the stocks by Regan, and proves immediately able to accept this mishap as a given, he says:

Nothing almost sees miracles
But misery. [II.2.161]

reworded freely: if "miraculous" improvements manifest themselves, then only out of dismal circumstances.

In fact, "up by way of down" forms the basis of the consulting situation. The need to ask for help often evokes a feeling of humiliation which clients understandably resist. The client has to acknowledge the authority of the consultant, as well as he has to acknowledge the fact that he could not solve his problem on his own. This is a major step for many people and a first step towards choosing to go "down". Thus, the very act of initiating a consulting process, even before anything has been done in that process, may lead to an improved situation for the client. Subsequently, the battle the client must fight to get "up" from the "down" position, within a complementary relationship with the consultant, can be acknowledged as the fruitful symmetrical relationship between client and consultant which we have also witnessed in *King Lear*.

2. Not accepting the monkey

In the course of *King Lear*, we have seen how powerful the contagious and absorbing effect of a dramatic situation is. A real tragedy leaves few people untouched. The tragedy is contagious: we see how, early in the play and in less than one hundred lines of text (I.1.25–I.1.120) King Lear creates a climate in which the entire kingdom will have to suffer. His need for flattery and the abdication of his responsibilities in that brief scene are the beginnings of a virus that spreads rapidly throughout the entire royal household. Edmund takes the opportunity to destroy his father and his brother, Goneril and Regan become corrupt with the power they obtained too easily and under false pretences, and so on. The tragedy draws others in as well: Edgar's development in particular demonstrates how a pitiable state such as King Lear's, and later Gloucester's, can make one feel involved and co-responsible. In the last scene, for instance, when Edgar relates how his father Gloucester died, he wonders, desperately and full of remorse, if things would have been different, had he revealed his true identity earlier (*Never—o fault!— revealed myself unto him*, V.3.190). In brief: the drama tempts the consultant. Commitment is certainly necessary, but it also carries the risk of making the consultant a party in the process. This is where the art of sharing responsibility is most subtle.

This brings us back to the theme of "the monkey on the back", which I addressed in the Introduction. Just as the manager feels responsible for the problems in his or her department, the consultant feels responsible for the problems of his or her client. There is a great risk of identifying oneself with the other's role: the manager identifies with his department, the consultant with the client. At that moment, the problems of others become one's own problems and the "monkey" is passed on. This monkey, or the problem, jumped on to the wrong back: that of the manager or the consultant who accepted the problem but did not have the necessary authority or leverage to solve it. The employee or client may be "rid" of the problem, but has also lost all control over the situation. A manager or consultant who does not accept the monkey, but only offers a judgement or advice and then asks what the other is going to do to solve the problem, takes full responsibility for his role, but no more than that.

3. Not offering advice

This method consists of a stronger version of the previous one: in the course of the consulting process that is *King Lear* we have witnessed how the advisers, despite being outsiders with an independent point of view and despite "knowing better" than the king, never undertake to offer advice. These very capable advisers never tell the king what they think he should or should not do. There are only two exceptions in the play: (1) in the first scene of Act I, Kent advises the king to reconsider his banning of Cordelia and (2) in the fourth Act, Edgar puts pressure on Gloucester, and even deceives him, to dissuade him from committing suicide. Interestingly, these two examples involve advice that is not acted upon but does evoke strong resistance from the person being advised. Moreover, Edgar, being Gloucester's son, is not even in a position to provide his father with independent advice.

The message of *King Lear* to "those who know better" is not to give in too easily to the temptation to put your advice forward by telling the client what is good for him. All too soon, one forgets that it is the client who best knows the situation and it is he or she who bears final responsibility for any decisions taken. What the client generally asks from the consultant is his or her judgement: new perceptions, suggestions and alternatives, which can be used to influence and modify his own strategy. A consultant can easily be tempted to go further than providing an interpretation or a personal judgement of the situation; for example, by offering advice. Offering unsolicited advice can, however, result in a conflict between consultant and client. Tempting though it is to demonstrate one's expertise in the form of "professional advice", if the client does not feel a need for it, or is not motivated to change, the only result will be unnecessary resistance.

Learning from King Lear

The client who is willing to share his dramatic story with the consultant has found himself in an unpleasant situation without having had the ability to resolve it. In this respect we have learned three lessons for the consultant: make sure the client accepts the situation ("up by way of down"), make sure you do not become part of the situation yourself ("do not accept the monkey"), and do not try to pull the client out of his situation at all costs ("do not offer advice"). Briefer still: something will have to come from nothing, if only because change is the normal course of events; in fact *not* changing is impossible for any living system.

EPILOGUE

"To serve him truly that will put me in trust"

(I.4.13)

T his English translation of *King Lear for Consultants and Managers* makes its appearance some eight years after I wrote the original Dutch-language text and about seven years after Scriptum Management published that book in The Netherlands. It is a matter of some excitement to me to be able to present the book to the English-speaking world. In the first place, of course, because William Shakespeare forms such a major part of the national heritage. The knowledge of his works is so widespread here that it is always a great pleasure to exchange impressions and discuss characters and story lines. But there is also another reason why it is interesting and exciting for me to see this English-language version published. And that is, that I am still active in the consulting profession, I still do my best to "serve him truly that will put me in trust", and I still assume the consulting role in a wide variety of settings. This publication, therefore, gives me the opportunity to revisit the themes set out in this book. I participated actively in the translation of the text and have reconsidered the themes in terms of the relevance they still have for my work.

What strikes me in the first place is the idea of responsible management, of assuming responsibility for one's own organizational role, and everything associated with that. In my own "role" as consultant I increasingly experience the assumption of responsibility as a so-called paradoxical intervention (Selvini Palazzoli *et al.*, 1975). I am very conscious of the fact that it is actually quite strange: taking responsibility for ensuring that the client takes his responsibility to as great a degree as possible. My responsibility centres on the responsibility of the client; therefore what occupies my attention is how the client relates to his own questions. Consequently, I frequently say to my clients, in so many words: "I would like to ask you, of yourself, to take full responsibility". This is, of course, an impossible request. Either the client assumes full responsibility and does so because I request it, whereby he or she actually acts under my responsibility, or the client does not do as I suggest, thereby taking personal responsibility for something else, whereby he or she still does as I have suggested, i.e., take full responsibility. In either case there is no escape for my poor client, who can only do as I say. I think that something of the magic of consulting and something of the impossible and counterintuitive effectiveness of consulting interventions lies in this paradox. In any case, for me consulting remains intriguing and I notice that I facilitate the taking of responsibility more consciously than was the case four or five years ago.

More generally, my impression is that the theme "responsibility" has a very fundamental relevance to working in organizations. Because it appears to be so obvious, we realize too little how essential and important it is that managers take responsibility. Without personal involvement, without a sense of the responsibility that adheres to a particular position, it is not possible to make things happen which would not have happened anyway; "anyway" meaning in this case: because someone else assumed responsibility. Without a real sense of involvement it is impossible to carry out one's role in a creative manner, to provide leadership and make a difference in the organization where one works. Taking responsibility demands more coordination and more perseverance than we think. There are all kinds of obstacles, internal barriers as well as external givens. Moreover, it is my experience that "assuming responsibility" is one of the most difficult things to learn. The assumption of responsibility relies very much on attitude and personality, which are very hard to change, even if the person involved is motivated to do so. Something else that I have noticed is how easily the sense of responsibility disappears when the situation is marked by stress and external pressure. It is precisely in such cases that taking responsibility for one's own situation and one's own output is so important. But we tend too quickly to throw in the towel and hope for divine intervention, or at least for another position more suited to our nature.

In all circumstances, except perhaps were I to be king, I must compare and adjust my own responsibility to the authority which I have. The responsibility which I assume must correspond with the responsibility which I have been given. In other words, there must be a correspondence between the sphere of influence or span of control on the one hand, and the mandate or authorization on the other. Perhaps it would be well to look more carefully into this difference: the difference between the responsibility required to carry out a function and the responsibility for a function once it has been carried out. In what follows I will, for the sake of convenience, discuss this in terms of the difference between "responsibility" and "mandate".

As we can read in many case studies and reports, the problem of responsibility without mandate, of a mandate which is less than the corresponding responsibility, is endemic in organizations. The desire for an "unburdened crawl towards" objectives and results and the wish to gather as many titles and as much status as possible without taking responsibility, manifests itself frequently even in the very highest echelons. Inadequate and inappropriate delegation of managerial tasks such as decision-making, problem solving, rewarding, and reprimanding are the result. This means that many middle managers carry an awful lot of responsibility in these areas but lack the corresponding mandate. Over-stressed middle management, so endemic in many organizations, is the result. This is why so many schools of organizational development attach such importance to the delegation of real authority, as expressed in many notions of "participation", "management development" and "empowerment".

Over the past few years I have increasingly also seen the opposite: mandate without responsibility. Managers change jobs with ever greater frequency. It has become a matter of course that managers go on to their next jobs within five years, and many do so even more quickly. If you haven't found something else within five years, your colleagues might even assume that you are doing something wrong. I also meet increasing numbers of interim managers in all kinds of vital positions, and increasing numbers of consultants working from a role concept which is hardly distinguishable from that of the interim manager. Consultants are being given more and more mandate as, for example, when they are linked to a manager as a "co-manager" for a period of time. What is worrying about these developments is that it is unlikely that a manager who performs a particular role for only a few years or, sometimes, even less than a year, will ever have to face the consequences of his own decisions.

It is difficult for me to estimate what is more damaging in terms of organizational effectiveness: responsibility without mandate, or mandate without responsibility. Perhaps the latter, because as a result of mandate without responsibility those who remain behind have no one who can be held accountable for the consequences. In the former case authority continues to rest in the hands of higher levels of management, so they can be called to account.

"Can you make no use of nothing, nuncle?" (I.4.128)

Interestingly, Shakespeare frequently writes about the situation in which someone is responsible for his decisions but lacks authorization, mandate or resources—without a mandate, but also without the possibility of shedding personal responsibility. Consider the unpleasant situations in which Lear, Gloucester, Kent and Edgar find themselves at different times during *King Lear*. Shakespeare seems frequently interested in responsibility without mandate; equally, he does not hold back from showing the results of acting from mandate alone, without the matching personal authority and sense of responsibility. Consider, for example, Richard II in the play of the same name, but also King Lear in the first act.

If we consider further the extremes of responsibility without mandate we end up with the question, how to "make something of nothing". Andrews (1991) demonstrates how Shakespeare broaches this topic in many places, and asks why there is so "much ado about nothing" in Shakespeare's dramas. He finds an answer in other tragedies such as *Coriolanus*, *Richard II* and *Timon of Athens*: time and again Shakespeare tells us in so many words that in order to lay strong foundations and establish a workable organization for a society in which we are responsible for our actions, we must first learn to cope with "nothing": with emptiness, ambiguity, indefiniteness and nihilism. We find a beautiful expression of this in Richard II's final monologue:

> Nor I, nor any man that but man is,
> With nothing shall be pleased, till he be eased
> With being nothing. [*Richard II*, V.5.39]

Making something of nothing makes me think of the creative process, of creating meaning in organizations. Is this not one of the most important tasks of management, to give meaning to what happens in an organization, to create a clearly delineated "something" from the "nothing" of unassimilated experience? That is the primary way in which a good manager can add value and become more than a "cost driver".

This "to make use of nothing" might also be at the core of why so many managers and consultants find inspiration in Shakespeare's texts, not least with regard to the art of leadership. I have encountered a number of examples in which consultants and managers are inspired by Shakespeare's texts to make "something" of providing personal authority and leadership to today's organizations, including

- reports of performances of Shakespeare's tragedies in a secure psychiatric hospital (Cox, 1992);
- a book about Shakespeare's "leadership lessons for today's managers" (Corrigan, 1999);
- a training programme in "inspirational leadership" conducted in Shakespeare's Globe, the place where Shakespeare's theatre once stood (Olivier, 2002).

What these wonderful examples have in common is the conviction that effective leadership can be influenced and learned, and that a good way of learning it might be to study and experience

Shakespeare's works. Though I am somewhat more pessimistic about the "learnability" of important competencies such as assuming responsibility and giving meaning to unassimilated experience, I agree wholeheartedly with the named authors that penetrating into the world of Shakespeare's tragedies will stimulate thought about these issues.

"This is the excellent foppery of the world" (I.2.118)

Since writing this book I have experienced great pleasure from attending performances of *King Lear*, and I have read many interpretations and discussed them with friends and colleagues. It surprised me that I could not encounter all of my own interpretation of Lear's tribulations in the many essays and reviews written about the tragedy. Under no circumstances would I wish to present my own interpretation as the only true or possible one, especially considering the enormous complexity of *King Lear*. Nevertheless, I started to wonder why Lear's lack of pride and his inability to assume responsibility for his role, as well as his wish to remain passive while retaining his full status as king, remain unnoticed by so many interpreters.

I suspect now that the fact that Lear's abdication of responsibilities has been so little discussed relates to the fact that it stems from an absence rather than a presence in his character. In tragedies critics have always sought some pride or a fatal weakness in the personality of the protagonist, and in my opinion these are much less relevant in *King Lear*. Lear's characteristic manner of leaving responsibility and initiative to those around him can easily be missed if we are looking for either over-confidence or a weak personality trait. I have often encountered interpretations in which the personality structure of the old king is beautifully dissected, until they reach the essential point: lack of a sense of responsibility. In order to illustrate this I would like to consider a highly respected and classic discourse on the tragedy, as contained in Bradley's *Shakespearean Tragedy* (1904). I select Bradley particularly because I heartily support all his points of view on the tragedy and the various characters in it. In his second lecture on *King Lear*, Bradley examines the characters of the key players, Lear's own contributions to the dramatic situations, and his fatal weaknesses. Bradley states emphatically that if Lear had not personally contributed to his own downfall, there could be no question of a tragedy: in that case the dramatic developments "would appear to us at best pathetic, at worst shocking, but certainly not tragic". Bradley begins with an interpretation which I share: he states that, in contrast to many tragedies, at the conclusion Lear "has for a long while been passive. We have long regarded him almost wholly as a sufferer, hardly at all as an agent". With that he suggests that "passivity" might well be his fatal weakness. But Bradley abandons that interpretation, as "passivity" is a mere "nothing", an absence of character, rather than an expression of hubris. Bradley does not wish to label Lear as irresponsible, because that would undo the "binding together of errors and calamities". Bradley therefore offers another suggestion: Lear's "presumptuous self-will, which in Greek Tragedy we have so often seen stumbling against the altar of Nemesis". This is, according to Bradley, a real tragic hubris. Certainly, but one that is so general that, as he says himself, it would apply to almost every tragedy!

My sense is that what happens to Bradley, and likewise to many others, shows an "excellent foppery" of Shakespeare interpreters, comparable to the "foppery" mentioned by Edmund, which allows us to ascribe all kinds of vicissitudes of fortune to

> ... the sun, the moon, and stars, as if we were villains of necessity, fools by heavenly compulsion, knaves, thieves, and treachers by spherical predominance; drunkards, liars, and adulterers by an enforced obedience of planetary influence ... [I.2.120]

Ascribing causes to vicissitudes of fortune is in fact quite comparable to ascribing responsibility to actions. It is therefore ironical and interesting to see that in the very case of Shakespeare's great tragedy, which concerns itself with the theme of responsibility, most commentators have been wrong-footed and tempted to neglect the abdication of responsibility, because this would deprive the play of its tragic character by making the protagonist insufficiently responsible for his own downfall!

"Now our joy, although the last, not least" (I.1.82)

I would like to express my thanks to three friends who made major contributions to the realization of this English translation. First to the translator, Corry Donner, who in fact took the initiative for this translation by initially coming up with the idea of translating the introduction. Then to my Dutch-Canadian colleague Nico Swaan, who subjected the translation to detailed and repeated scrutiny, particularly with regard to sentence structure and technical relevance. And finally to the Spanish psychiatrist, Carmen Clemente, who reviewed and commented on the translations in every phase of the writing process.

Also, I would like to mention four other professionals, who in 1996 helped me with the original text: theatre director Erik Vos, drama professor Wiebe Hogendoorn, psychotherapist Ric Oostburg, and career consultant Gerard Wijers.

London, November 5, 2003
Erik de Haan
erik.dehaan@ashridge.org.uk
http://home.hetnet.nl/~e.de.haan

REFERENCES

Andrews, J. F. (1991). Editor's introduction to King Lear. In: J. F. Andrews (Ed.), *King Lear*. New York: Doubleday.

Aristotle (4th century BC) [1920]. *Peri Poietikes*. [*Aristotle on the Art of Poetry*, I. Bywater (Trans.)]. Oxford: Oxford University Press.

Bell, C. R., & Nadler, L. (Eds.) (1979). *Clients & Consultants*. Houston: Gulf Publishing Company.

Berne, E. (1964). *Games People Play*. New York: Grove Press.

Block, P. (1981). *Flawless Consulting*. San Diego: University Associates.

Bradley, A. C. (1904). *Shakespearean Tragedy—Lectures on* Hamlet, Othello, King Lear, Macbeth. London: Macmillan.

Corrigan, P. (1999). *Shakespeare on Management—leadership lessons for today's managers*. London: Kogan Page.

Cox, M. (Ed.) (1992). *Shakespeare comes to Broadmoor—"The actors are come hither"—The performance of tragedy in a secure psychiatric hospital*. London: Jessica Kingsley.

De Haan, E. (2001). *Leren met collega's*. Assen: Van Gorcum.

Foucault, M. (1985). *Discourse and Truth. The problematization of parrhesia*, Lecture series edited by J. Pearson. Evanston, Illinois: Northwestern University Press.

Harrison, R. (1997). A time for letting go. *Organization Development Journal*, 15(2): 79–86.

Kolb, D. A. (1984). *Experiential Learning—Experience as the Source of Learning and Development.* Englewood Cliffs, NJ: Prentice Hall.

Leary, T. (1957). *Interpersonal Diagnosis of Personality.* New York: The Ronald Press.

Olivier, R. (2002). *Inspirational Leadership—Henry V and the muse of fire.* Rollinsford, NH: Spiro Press.

Oncken Jr., W., & Wass, D. L. (1974). Management Time: who's got the monkey? *Harvard Business Review,* Nov.–Dec., pp. 75–80.

Putnam, A. O. (1979) *Managing Resistance.* In: C. R. Bell & L. Nadler (Eds.), *Clients & Consultants.* Houston: Gulf Publishing Company.

Rose, G. J. (1969). King Lear and the use of humor in treatment. *Journal of the American Psychoanalytic Association,* 17: 927–940.

St Augustine (398) [1961]. *Confessiones* (English edition: *Confessions*). London: Penguin.

Selvini Palazzoli, M., Cechin, G., Prata, G., & Boscolo, L. (1975). *Paradosso e controparadosso.* Milan: Feltrinelli. [English edition (1978) *Paradox and Counterparadox.* New York: Jason Aronson].

Tichy, N. M., & Devanna, M. A. (1986). *The Transformational Leader.* New York: Wiley.

Shakespeare, W. (1608) [1928]. *King Lear.* In: K. Muir (Ed.), *The Arden Edition.* London/New York: Routledge.

Verhagen, B. (1928). *Dramaturgie.* Amsterdam: Van Munster.

INDEX

Andrews, J. F., 59, 63
appreciative inquiry, 16
Aristotle, 36, 63

Beckett, xii
Bell, C. R., xii, 63
Berne, E., 28, 63
Block, P., xi, 9, 20, 31, 50, 63
Boscolo, L., 45, 56, 64
Bradley, A. C., xii, 60–61, 63

catharsis, 36
Cechin, G., 45, 56, 64
change, 2, 17, 26, 29–31, 33–34,
    39–40, 42–43, 46–47, 51, 53–54,
    57
  and remaining the same, 43, 45,
    47
  transformational, 30
compassion, 27, 31, 35, 39, 42, 49, 51
consulting, 1–2, 5–6, 8–9, 15–17,
    19–20, 23, 26, 30, 33–34, 41–43,
    45, 47–51, 53

and advice, 2, 12–13, 18, 23–24,
    28–29, 30–31, 39–40, 53–54,
    55
and letting go, 2, 34, 41–42
and organizational development,
    57
and speaking one's mind, 2, 9
and state of mind, 1–2, 16
as exploration, 2, 8, 15–16, 23, 25
as facilitation, 2, 24, 33–34, 47,
    56
co-dependency, 42
contract, 12, 15–16, 24, 48
converse of, 20
evaluation, 40, 43, 45–47
expertise, 5, 8, 12, 21, 16, 24–25,
    31, 53
intervention, xii, 16, 21, 23–24, 26,
    30, 33–34, 43, 56
key issues in/key perspectives of,
    xiii, 1–2, 7, 15, 23, 33
literature, 5, 24, 30
management, xi, 1, 5, 30, 47, 50

phase(s), xii, 1–2, 7–8, 12–13,
    15–16, 20–21, 23–25, 29–31,
    33–34, 39–42, 46–47, 49
professional standards of, 20–21,
    53
relationship, 2, 7, 17, 24, 29, 41
resistance to, 26, 30–31, 36, 53
roles, 8, 16, 25, 28, 55
self-monitoring and self-
    directing, 2, 25–26, 33
Corrigan, P., 59, 63
Cox, M., 59, 63
creativity, 19, 31, 59
crisis, xii, 23, 26–27, 29–30

De Haan, E., 24, 63
denouement, xii, 33
Devanna, M. A., 30, 64
dramatic situation(s), xi, 5, 30, 52

flattery, 9–10, 18–20, 36, 52
Foucault, M., 9, 63

Harrison, R., 42, 63
hybris, 4

Kolb, D. A., 24, 64

Leary, T., 51, 64

management
    and creating meaning, 59
    interim, 58
    lead/leadership, xi, 5, 24, 56, 59
Marlowe, C., 4

Nadler, L., 63
nothing, 3, 10–11, 19, 47, 50–51, 54,
    58–59, 61

Olivier, R., 59, 64
Oncken, W. (Jr.), 5, 64

paradox, 43, 45, 56
parrhesia, 9

peripeteia, xii, 23, 26, 29
Prata, G., 45, 56, 64
pride, 4, 60
Putnam, A. O., 31, 64

relationship
    symmetrical and complementary,
        24–26, 28–29, 31, 52, 56
Renaissance, 4
responsibility, xiii, 5, 12, 20–21, 31,
        39–40, 42, 47, 50, 56, 58,
        60–61
    and authority, 53, 57–58, 59
    and mandate, 57–58
    giving and taking of, 37, 39–40,
        50–51, 52–53, 57
    learning of, 57, 60
role(s), 4–5, 16, 19, 24–27, 29, 35,
        42–43, 47–49, 51–53, 55–56, 58,
        60
Rose, G. J., 20, 64

St Augustine, 1, 64
Selvini Palazzoli, M., 45, 56, 64
Shakespeare, W., xi, 3–5, 37, 45, 55,
        58–61, 64
    Coriolanus, 59
    Hamlet, 3, 5, 29
    King Lear, v, xi–xiii, 3–5, 9, 13, 17,
        25–26, 30–31, 34, 36, 40, 43,
        47–50, 52–55, 58, 60
    Macbeth, 3, 5
    Othello, 3, 5
    Richard II, 59
    Timon of Athens, 59
symptom(s), 51

Tichy, N. M., 30, 64
tragic impotence, 17
transform/transformation, 28, 30,
        36, 45

Verhagen, B., 3, 64

Wass, D. L., 5, 64